KB090595

여행 · 항공 · 호텔 · F&B 분야의 실무자들을 위한

Global Service English

Jin-oh Kim

BAEKSAN

머리말　　　　　　　　　　# Preface

국가별 장벽이 없는 글로벌시대를 즐기기 위해서는 언어 소통이 무엇보다 필요하다. 성능 좋은 번역 어플리케이션을 활용하면 해외 여행도 큰 어려움 없이 가능하겠지만, 현지 외국인들과 눈을 마주 보고 소통하며 얻을 수 있는 즐거운 여행 경험은 할 수 없을 것이다.

이 책은 여행의 Outbound와 Inbound에 필요한 필수 영어 표현을 담고 있다. 뿐만 아니라 저자가 외국인들과 업무상 주고 받은 이메일도 일부 수록했으며 이것은 외국인들이 실제 사용하는 언어를 보여준다.

해외자유여행, 해외비즈니스 출장, 관광서비스 분야, 외국인 서비스 실무, 그리고 F&B 분야에 관련된 분들에게 도움이 되는 영어교재이다.

Communication을 위한 영어를 가장 효과적으로 습득할 수 있는 방법 중에 하나는 영어를 영어로 Rephrase하는 방식이다. 이 교재 활용 및 학습 방법의 포인트가 바로 주요 Rephrase 부분에 있다.

저자가 지난 20여 년간 해외 각국 비즈니스 출장과 국내외 국제행사 및 외국인 통역 업무를 토대로 필수 영어 표현을 쉽게 정리했으며, 교재에 들어간 모든 사진 자료는 저자가 현지에서 직접 찍은 것이다.

아무쪼록 이 책을 접하는 모든 분들이 큰 성취감을 맛보길 기원하며, 부족한 가운데서도 이 책 집필에 힘을 준 소중한 가족, 대학 제자들 그리고 백산출판사 편집부에 깊은 감사를 드린다.

화이트 크리스마스 날 오후, 서재에서…

저자 김 진 오

차 례

Contents

Chapter 4. Situational Conversation • • • 135

CHAPTER

1

Greetings

CHAPTER
1 Greetings

The greetings good morning, good afternoon, good evening are used at different times of the day to greet people.

"Good evening" is often used generally when the sun has set.

"Good night" is not a greeting. It is used when leaving a place or group of people.

Thank you and good night! and see you tomorrow. When people meet in the United States, it is customary for them to shake hands. A handshake should be firm and usually lasts for about two to three seconds — which allows enough time to say "Nice to meet you." "Don't mention it" is another way of saying "You're welcome." The phrase "You are welcome" is more formal. However, responses such as Don't mention it/No problem/Happy to help are informal ways of responding to a thank you.

[Useful expressions Used by Staff]

1. Magic Words Used by Staff

- Please

- Thank You

- Excuse Me

- Pardon Me

- Sorry

2. For Addressing Individual Guests

If you do not know the guest's name, address him or her as:

- Sir

- Madam

- Sir & Madam

If you are addressing children, address them as:

- Young Man/Young Gentleman

- Young Lady

- Note: Refrain from using "KIDS" when addressing children

3. For Addressing a group of guests. When addressing a group of guests, use:

- Gentlemen

- Ladies

- Ladies and Gentlemen

4. Standard Greeting Used by Staff

In greeting guest, be warm, friendly and professional.

Do say:

- "Good Morning, Sir/Madam."

- "Good Afternoon, Sir/Madam."

- "Good Evening, Sir/Madam."

- Never be too personal

Do not say:

- "Hi."

- "Hello."

- "Yes?"

In the exchange of greetings, use:

"How are you today Mr. (surname)?

        this morning Ms. (surname)?

        this afternoon Mrs. (surname)?

        this evening, Miss. (surname)?"

For new arrivals, you can add:

"Have a pleasant stay with us, Sir/Madam."

"I hope you'll enjoy your stay with us, Sir/Madam."

5. Standard expression While Offering of service/help:

In offering your assistance, the phrases are:

- "May I help you, Sir/Madam?"
- "May I be of service to you, Sir/Madam?"

Words in response

In response to something said positively, the phrase is:

"I'm glad to hear that."

In response to something negative e.g. bad news, the phrase to use is:

"I'm sorry to hear that."

In response to guest greeting you with "How are you today?" say:

"Fine, thank you."

"Very well, thank you."

6. While Answering a guest or client's call. In answering to a guest's call, the phrases are:

- "Yes Mr (surname) / (Sir/Madam), may I help you?"
- "Yes Mr (surname) / (Sir/Madam), may I be of any assistance?"

Do not ignore a client by continuing with what you are doing, even if you are very busy.

- "I'll be with you in a moment."
- "I'll only be a few moments."
- "I'll be right back."
- "I'll be right with you."
- Do not say - "Wait a minute."

Upon attending to the guest, immediately say:

- "Sorry to keep you waiting, Sir/Madam."
- "Sorry to have kept you waiting, Sir/Madam."

7. When a guest requests for something Do not go away to fetch it in silence, response by saying:

- "Certainly Sir/Madam."
- "Yes Sir/Madam, it's my pleasure."
- "Of course Sir/Madam, I'll be happy to do it."

When guest asks for something which you cannot provide Say:

- "I'm very sorry, we have run out of."
- "Unfortunately, we don't seem to have it at the moment."
- "I regret Sir/Madam, we have sold all out."
- "I'm afraid we do not have."

- Always remember to follow that up with an alternative solution as a sign of your desire to help.
- Do not say: "No, we don't have it."

8. When guest asks for something which you are not sure you can provide, do not say:

- "I don't think we have it."
- "It is not handled by this department."
- Instead answer honestly: "If you wait for a moment, Sir/Madam, I'll try to find out."

9. To say when guest thanks you:

Always reply with a big smile

- "Please don't mention it."
- "My pleasure."
- "You're most welcome."
- "Not at all. I'm glad I am able to help."
- "Glad to be of service."
- Do not say: "Never mind."
- Or worse, make no reply at all.

10. To say When guest apologizes by saying "sorry"

- Do reply - "That's quite all right."
- Do not reply - "Never mind."

11. To say When Giving way to guests

- When guests pass you, remember to let guests go first.
- Do say: "After you, Sir/Madam."

12. Informal, friendly context - first name

Formal first meetings, esp. elderly people - title + last name

Mr. Ms. Mrs. Mx.

Don't address people using

- First & last name

- Last name only

- Sir or ma'am if you know the name

UNIT 1

Introducing yourself

1. I'm (name) from (company or country)

I'm Rina from ABC company.

I'm Gunn from South Korea.

2. My name is (name). I'm a (position).

My name is Rina. I'm a marketing manager.

My name is Gunn. I'm a student.

3. I'm (name). I work as a (position) at (company)

I'm Tom. I work as a marketing manager at Global Korea Co.

I'm Gunn. I work as a CEO at Global Korea Co.

Dialogue 1

A: Hello! I'm Gunn. I'm your new <u>neighbor</u>.

B: Hello! I'm David. Welcome to the <u>neighborhood</u>.

 Dialogue 2

A: Hello! I don't think we've met. My name is Bill

　And I'm the head of <u>management</u> of this apartment.

B: Hello! I'm Amy. I've just moved into this apartment in this city.

 Dialogue 3

A: Allow me to introduce myself. My name is Gunn Kim

　And I am the hotel manager.

B: Hello! Mr. Kim. I'm Amy Lewis. I'm the <u>representative</u> of K-Travel.

Neighbor : a person who lives next to you or near you.

Neighborhood : the area that you are in or the area near a particular place.

Representative : a person who has been chosen for a group of people.

Dialogue 4

A: Mr. Ritchie! I'll see you at next meeting.

B: Ms. Park! I'll <u>look forward to</u> that.

Dialogue 5

A: Bye, Mom! I'll see you next month.

B: Bye, dear! Drive carefully!

Dialogue 6

A: Bye-bye, Amy! Let's have lunch again very soon.

B: Bye, Sue, that's good idea! I'll <u>give</u> you a <u>ring</u>.

Look forward to : to be thinking with pleasure about something that is going to happen.
(because you expect to enjoy it.)
Ex) We are really looking forward to seeing you again.
Give (somebody) a ring : to make a phone call to somebody.

Dialogue 7

A: Good bye, Mom! Thanks for driving me to the station.

B: Bye, Tom! Have a safe trip!

UNIT 2

Greetings

Formal Greetings arriving

- Good morning / afternoon / evening.

- Hello (name), how are you?

- Good day Sir / Madam (very formal)

Respond to a formal greeting with another formal greeting.

- Good morning Mr. Kim.

- Hello Ms. Park. How are you today?

Informal Greetings

- Hi / Hello?
- How are you?
- How are you doing?
- What's up? (very informal)

Informal Greetings After a Long Time

(If you haven't seen a friend or family member for a long time, use one these informal greetings to mark the occasion.)

- It's great to see you!
- How have you been?
- Long time, no see.
- How are you doing these days?

Formal Greetings: Departing

(Use these greetings when you say goodbye at the end of the day. These greetings are appropriate for work and other formal situations.)

- It was a pleasure seeing you.
- Goodbye.

- Goodnight.

Informal Greetings: Departing

(Use these greetings when saying goodbye in an informal situation.)

- Nice seeing you!
- Goodbye / Bye
- See you later
- Later (very informal)

Example

1. How are you? / How are you doing?

- Very well, thank you. And you? (formal)

- Fine / Great (informal)

2. What's up?

- Not much.

- I'm just (watching TV, hanging out, cooking etc.)

Dialogue 1

A: James, what's up?

B: Hi Olivia. Nothing much. I'm just <u>hanging out</u>.

What's up with you?

A: It's a good day. I'm feeling fine.

B: How is your sister?

A: Oh, fine. Not much has changed.

B: Well, I have to go. Nice seeing you!

A: See you later!

 Dialogue 2

A: Oh, hello John. How are you doing?

B: I'm well. Thanks for asking. How are you?

A: I can't <u>complain</u>. Life is <u>treating</u> me well.

B: That's good to hear.

hang out : to spend a lot of time in a place

complain : unhappy or not satisfied about somebody/something

treat : behave in a particular way towards somebody/something

A: Good to see you again. I need to go to my doctor's <u>appointment</u>.

B: Nice seeing you.

A: See you later.

 Dialogue 3

A: Good morning.

B: Good morning. <u>How are you</u>?

A: I'm very well thank you. And you?

B: I'm fine. Thank you for asking.

A: Do you have a meeting this morning?

B: Yes, I do. Do you have a meeting <u>as well</u>?

A: Yes. Well. It was a pleasure seeing you.

B: Goodbye.

---

appointment : a formal arrangement to meet or visit somebody at a particular time

How are you : It is a conventional greeting used to ask about someone's Health and welfare.

   Ex) "Hello, Tom! How are you?"

   "Hello, Jane! I'm fine, thanks. And you?"

As well (As) : in addition to somebody / something; too

   Ex) Are they coming as well?

   They sell books as well as magazines.

   She is a talented musician as well as being a photographer.

Dialogue 4

James: Good morning, Professor Austin. How are you doing?

Professor Austin: Good morning, James. I am doing well. And you?

James: I'm great, thank you. This is my friend Emma. She is thinking about <u>applying</u> to this college. She has a few questions. Would you mind telling us about the <u>process</u>, please?

Professor Austin: Hello, Emma! It's a pleasure to meet you. I'm more than happy to speak with you. Please <u>stop by</u> my office next week.

Emma: It's a pleasure to meet you, professor. Thank you so much for helping us.

Professor Austin: Don't mention it. Hopefully, I will be able to answer your questions!

Apply : to make a formal request, usually in writing, for something such as a job, permission for something, a place at a university, etc.
   Ex) apply to a company/university
Process : a series of things that are done
Stop by : to make a short visit somewhere.
   Ex) Could you stop by the store on the way home for some bread.

Dialogue 5

Brown: Mr. Parker, did you meet Mr. Lee yet?

Parker: No, not yet.

Brown: <u>Why don't you</u> meet each other now, then?

        Mr. Parker, this is Mr. Lee. Mr. Lee, this is Mr. Parker

Parker: How do you do, Mr. Lee?

Lee: Nice to meet you, Mr. Parker.

Dialogue 6

A: How's it going?

B: I'm well, thank you. <u>How about</u> yourself?

A: I'm fine, too.

B: That's good.

How/what about···?: used when asking for information about Somebody / something.

               used to make a suggestion.

                 Ex) How about Ruth? Have you heard from her?

                    How about going for a walk?

                    What about a break.

Dialogue 7

A: Hi! Mr. Kim, long time no see!

B: Mr. Brown! <u>I haven't seen you for ages!</u>

How have you been?

A: Keeping busy, very busy.

B: That's great. Looks like you are the only person not affected by the

recession.

 Dialogue 8

A: We have been talking for about an hour, but <u>we haven't met yet</u>,

Have we?

B: No. my name is John.

A: Thomas here. Nice to meet you.

B: Same here.

I haven't seen you for ages! : Long time no see!
We haven't met yet : we haven't told each other names yet.

Dialogue 9

A: Hi, John! Are you not driving to work today?

B: Hi, Sue! No, I'm going by train. My car <u>broke down</u> today.

 Dialogue 10

A: Hi Mark! Where are you <u>off to</u> so early?

B: Hi Tim! I'm starting work early today so that I can finish early.

 Dialogue 11

A: Hi there, Bob! I haven't seen you for a long time.

<u>Have you been away</u>?

B: Hi John, Yes. I've been working in L.A.

Break down : (of a machine or vehicle) to stop working because of fault

Off to : going to (away from a place)

Have you been away : it means something like I have been somewhere else for some time,
but now I have returned.

CHAPTER 2

Airlines

CHAPTER

2 Airlines

An airline is a company that provides air transport services for traveling passengers and freight.

UNIT 1

Airline Reservation

An "airline reservation" is a legal contract whereby an airline undertakes, in exchange for a certain amount of money, to provide a seat to a specific passenger by plane on a specific flight from one specified airport to another.

As an example, somebody may make an airline reservation with British Airways to fly from London to Budapest on flight BA0055 on the 25th April 2022, scheduled to leave London Heathrow at 1905 and arrive in Budapest at 0650.

Dialogue 1

A: Korean Airline, May I help you?

B: I'd like to make a <u>reservation</u> a ticket to Auckland, NZ.

Dialogue 2

A: Asiana Airline, how can I help you?

B: Ok, I'd like to <u>book</u> a ticket to London.

Reservation: an arrangement for a seat on a plane or train, a room in a hotel, etc.
to be kept for you.

Book = reserve = make a reservation

Ex) I'm sorry, we're fully booked.

Dialogue 3

A: I'd like to book a flight to New York.

B: When do you want to travel?

A: Next month, the 13th.

B: Would you like a return ticket?

A: Yes, I'm coming back on the 28th.

Dialogue 4

A: Are there any planes to Sydney on Monday?

B: <u>Hold on</u> a second please, I'll check.

A: By the way, I don't want a night flight.

B: There's a <u>flight</u> at 10:30 a.m.

A: When am I supposed to check in?

B: You must be at the airport before 8:30.

Hold on: to tell somebody to wait or stop. (used on the phone as well)

　　　Ex) Hold on! This is the right road.

　　　Can you hold on? I'll see if he's here.

Flight: a journey by air.

　　　Ex) We met on a flight from London to Paris.

　　　We're booked on the same flight

Dialogue 5

A: Hello.

B: Hi. What time is the next flight to San Francisco?

A: At 4:00 this afternoon.

B: I'd like to buy a ticket.

A: Ok. What's your name?

B: Gunn Kim.

A: Could you spell it for me?

B: Sure. Gunn is G-U-N-N and Kim is spelled K-I-M.

A: And what's your phone number?

B: Area code (063) 222-1234.

A: Ok. Would you like a window or aisle seat?

B: Window seat please.

A: How would you like to pay for your ticket?

B: I'd like to pay by credit card.

I like to VS I'd like to
I like is used when you say about something you like generally.
    Ex) I like apples, I like coffee, etc.
I would like is used when you say about what you like at current situation.
    Ex) I would like coffee, I would like noodles" etc.
Aisle: a passage between rows of seats in a train, plane, etc.

A: Ok. Here is your ticket.

B: Thanks.

Dialogue 6

A: Hello, British airway. How may I help you?

B: I would like to book a flight.

A: I can help you with that. Where are you traveling to?

B: I am traveling to Paris.

A: What date will you be traveling?

B: On July 4th.

A: Would you <u>prefer</u> a morning or an afternoon flight?

B: <u>I'd rather</u> fly in the morning.

Prefer: to like one thing or person better than another
　　　　To choose one thing rather than something else because you like it better.
　　　　Ex) 'Coffee or tea?' 'I'd prefer tea, thanks.'
　　　　　　I much prefer jazz to rock music.
Would rather...(than): would prefer to.
　　　　Ex) She'd rather die than give a speech.
　　　　　　'Do you mind if I smoke?'
　　　　　　'Well, I'd rather you didn't'

A: Well, I have you booked on a flight that will <u>fit</u> your schedule. The tickets will arrive by email in a couple of days.

 Dialogue 7

A: Hello, I'd like to book a ticket to Rome, Italy Please.

B: Alright. Would you like a <u>round trip</u> or a one-way ticket?

A: I'd like a round trip ticket. I'd like to leave by July 3th and return by September 7th.

B: Got it. And which class would you like to fly?

A: Economy class please.

B: OK.

Fit: to be the right shape and size for somebody/something.
   Make suitable.
      Ex) My jacket fits well.
         His experience fitted him perfectly for the job.
Round trip: a journey to a place and back again.

Dialogue 8

A: Northwestern Airlines, Can I help you?

B: Hi, I'd like to <u>confirm</u> my flight reservation please.

A: May I have your name and phone Number please?

B: My name is Tom Radford and my phone number is 234-5678.

A: When are you leaving?

B: On April 2nd.

A: And your <u>destination</u>?

B: Incheon.

Confirm and reconfirm: check again that something is correct or as previously arranged.

Destination: ex) tourist destination, final destination.

UNIT 2

Airport Check in

Check-in is usually the first procedure for a passenger when arriving at an airport. To check in at the airport, find the terminal for your airline and approach the check-in counter. Once you reach the counter, let the worker know if you will be checking any bags, and give the worker your identification so they can print your boarding pass.

Dialogue 1

A: Excuse me, where is the check-in counter for Korean Airlines?

B: You need to go back to terminal 1.

A: I see. May I ask what terminal I am in?

B: You are currently in terminal 2.

A: Oh, I see. Is there some kind of <u>shuttle</u> that I can <u>ride</u> to go there?

It is quite far from here.

B: Yes, you can use the shuttle bus right here.

A: Thank you very much.

Shuttle: a plane, bus or train that travels regularly between two places.

    Ex) Shuttle bus, Shuttlecock, Space shuttle.

Ride: to seat on something such as a bicycle, horse etc.

    Ex) ride a horse, I'll give you a ride.

Dialogue 2

A: good morning. Can I have your ticket please?

B: Here you are.

A: <u>would you like</u> a window or an aisle seat?

B: An aisle seat please.

A: Do you have any baggage?

B: Yes, this is my <u>luggage</u> and this one is <u>carry-on bag</u>.

A: Ok, here's your <u>boarding pass</u> and baggage claim tag.

Have a nice flight.

B: Thank you.

Would you like~
    EX) Would you like to have coffee? / What would you like?
Luggage = baggage
Carry-on bag: small bags that you can keep with you on an aircraft.
Boarding pass: It identifies the passenger, the flight number, and the date and scheduled
                time for departure.

Dialogue 3

A: Good morning, where are you flying to?

B: Good morning. I am flying to Seattle.

A: Do you have your tickets?

B: Here is my ticket.

A: How many people are travelling?

B: Two people.

A: Can I have your passports?

B: Sure. Here they are.

A: Would you like a window or an aisle seat?

B: I would be very happy If we can get an aisle seat.

A: Alright, I'll put you near the restrooms too.

B: Wonderful, thanks.

A: Sure, are you checking in any bags?

B: Yes, this suitcase and my backpack.

A: Please put them on the scale, one at a time, please.

B: Sure. And by the way, I have a layover in London.

Do I have to pick up my luggage there?

Scale: ex) Weighing scale, scale of fish, teeth scaling.

Layover: short stay at a place in the middle of a flight trip (less than 24hours)

Stopover: Same as layover but stay more than 24hours

A: No, you will pick them up in Seattle.

Here is your boarding pass.

B: Thank you for your help, have a good day.

A: Thank you, have a nice flight.

Dialogue 4

A: Good afternoon! Where are you flying to today?

B: San Francisco.

A: May I have your passport, please?

B: Here you go.

A: Are you checking any bags?

B: Yes, Just this one.

A: OK, please place your bag on the scale.

B: I have a stopover in Seattle - do I need to pick up my luggage there?

A: No, it'll go straight through to San Francisco.

Here is your boarding pass − your flight leaves from gate 123 and it'll begin boarding at 2:20pm Your seat number is 24A.

B: Thanks.

UNIT 3

Boarding a plane

How to Board a plane?

Step 1. Print your boarding pass and check your luggage.

Step 2. Head to <u>security</u>.

Step 3. Find your gate/terminal.

Step 4. Hang out and wait for your plane.

Step 5. Wait for the announcement to board.

Security: a place at an airport where you go after your passport has been checked so that officials can find out if you are carrying illegal items.

Step 6. Get your boarding pass checked at the boarding gate.

Step 7. Walk down the <u>hallway</u> that leads up to your plane.

Step 8. Enter the <u>aircraft</u>.

Step 9. <u>Stow</u> your carry-on items.

Step 10. Get <u>settled in</u>.

Hallway: corridor, passage.
Aircraft: vehicle that can fly (Airplane).
    Cf) hovercraft.
Stow: put something in a safe place
    Ex) She found a seat, stowed her backpack and sat down.
Settle in: feel comfortable in a place.

Going through Security

Step 1. Please <u>step</u> through the scanner − Asked when you are passing through <u>metal detectors</u> at the airport.

Step 2. Please step to the side − Asked if a security officer need to question you further.

Step 3. Please raise your arms to the side - Asked when you are inside a scanner.

Step 4. Empty your pockets, please.

Step 5. Please take off your shoes and belt.

Step 6. Please take any electronic devices out of your bag.

Step: ex) watch(mind) your step!, step by step,
   He stepped out of the office.
   she moved a step closer to me.
Metal detector: electronic device that is used to see if people are
   hiding metal objects such as weapons.

Dialogue 1

A: Please step through the scanner.

B: (beep, beep, beep) <u>What's wrong?</u>

A: Please step to the side.

B: Certainly.

A: Do you have any coins in your pocket?

B: No, but I have some keys.

A: Ah, that's the problem. Put your keys in this <u>bin</u> and walk through the scanner again.

B: Ok

A: Excellent. No problem. Remember to <u>unload</u> your pockets before you go through security next time.

B: I'll do that. Thank you.

A: Have a nice trip.

What's wrong: What's the matter?, What happened?
Bin: a container that you put something in.
     Rubbish(waste) bin, bread bin, overhead bin
Unload: remove things from a vehicle or ship

At the duty free shop

DFS is located at the international terminals. Duty free shopping means shopping without paying duties or taxes.

 Dialogue 2

A: Hello, I'd like to buy this liquor. Is it good for a souvenir?

B: Yes, very popular.

A: I see. I'll take two bottles, then.

B: Very well, sir A: Can you wrap them separately if possible?

B: Certainly, No problem. Pay in cash or card?

A: Do you accept Master card?

B: Of course. Could you show me your boarding pass?

A: Alright. Here you go.

B: Thank you. Would you like to pay in Korean won or dollars? You can choose.

A: Pay in dollar, please.

B: Ok, here you are. Thank you for shopping with us, and have a safe trip!

A: Thank you, have a great day.

When and how we board

Most flights start boarding 30 - 50 minutes before scheduled <u>departure</u>, but the exact time <u>depends on</u> your <u>destination</u> and plane. Boarding ends 15 minutes before departure. If you're not on board, we may <u>reassign</u> your seat to another passenger. You will not be allowed to board once the doors close.

—American Airlines—

Departure: Departure time

    Ex) We sat in the departure lounge waiting for our flight to be called

    Cf) arrival.

Depend on

    Ex) It depends.

        It depends on the weather.

        Depend on it (=you can be sure)

        I don't want to depend too much on my parents

Destination

    Ex) popular tourist destination like the Bahamas

        Our luggage was checked all the way through to our final destination

Reassign: give somebody a different duty, position

Pre boarding announcement

Good evening passengers. This is the pre-boarding <u>announcement</u> for flight KE123 to London. We are now inviting those passengers with small children, and any passengers requiring special <u>assistance</u>, to begin boarding at this time. Please have your boarding pass and <u>identification</u> ready. Regular boarding will begin in <u>approximately</u> ten minutes. Thank you.

Final boarding announcement

This is the final boarding call for passengers Jeff and Thomas Cruise booked on flight KE156 to San Francisco. Please proceed to gate 5 immediately. The final checks are being completed and the <u>captain</u> will order for the doors of the aircraft to close in approximately five minutes. I repeat. This is the final boarding call for Jeff and Thomas Cruise. Thank you.

Announcement: make an announcement, public announcement.
Assistance: help or support.
            Ex) technical/economic assistance.
Identification: ex) ID card, Personal Identification Number (PIN).
Approximately: about, around, roughly.
Captain: a person who is in charge of an airplane.

Pre flight announcement

Ladies and gentlemen, welcome aboard Flight KE001 with service from Incheon to San Francisco. We are currently third in line for <u>take-off</u> and are expected to be in the air in approximately seven minutes. We ask that you please <u>fasten your seatbelts</u> at this time and secure all baggage <u>underneath</u> your seat or in the <u>overhead compartments</u>. We also ask that your seats and table trays are in the upright position for take-off. Please <u>turn off</u> all personal electronic devices, including laptops and cell phones. Smoking is <u>prohibited</u> for the <u>duration</u> of the flight. Thank you for choosing Korean Airlines. Enjoy your flight.

Take off: leave the ground and begin to fly
      Ex) the plane took off an hour late.
      Cf) Landing.

Fasten your seatbelt please.
Underneath: below Overhead: above your head.
Compartment: bin , container.
Turn off: turn off the light.
Prohibit: forbid. Stop something from being done by law.
Duration: the length of time.

Captain's announcement

Good afternoon passengers. This is your captain speaking.

First, I'd like to welcome everyone on British Airway. We are currently <u>cruising</u> at an <u>altitude</u> of 33,000 feet at an airspeed of 400 miles per hour. The time is 1:25 pm. The weather looks good and with the tailwind on our side we are expecting to land in London approximately fifteen minutes <u>ahead of</u> schedule. The weather in London is clear and sunny, with a high of 25 degrees for this afternoon. If the weather <u>cooperates</u> we should get a great view of the city as we <u>descend</u>. The <u>cabin crew</u> will be coming around in about twenty minutes time to offer you a light snack and <u>beverage</u>, and the <u>inflight</u> movie will begin shortly after that.

I'll talk to you again before we reach our destination. Until then, sit back, relax and enjoy the rest of the flight.

Cruise: a journey on a ship to a number of places / Cruise ship, Cruising speed
Altitude: the height above sea level.
Ahead of: earlier than …, ahead of time,
Cooperate: to be helpful or to work together with somebody in order to achieve something.
Descend: go down from a higher to a lower level.
Cabin crew: flight attendant,
Beverage: any type of drink except water.
Inflight: Inflight service (Inflight meal, Inflight movie etc.)

UNIT 4

Inflight service

Dialogue 1

A: Would you like something to drink?

B: Yes, what kind of drink do you have?

A: We have tea, coffee, and apple juice.

B: coffee please.

Dialogue 2

A: We have beef and fish.

Which would you like?

B: I'll have fish, please.

A: here you are.

B: Thank you.

Dialogue 3

A: Can I help you?

B: I think I have a headache.

Could you give me some medicine?

A: Yes, I'll bring you a pill for the headache.

B: Thank you very much.

Dialogue 4

A: Would you like to order any <u>duty free goods</u>?

B: Yes, please. Can I pay by credit card?

A: Yes, all major credit cards are accepted but purchases must not exceed six hundred US dollars.

B: Ok, Umm… I'd like this bottle of scotch whiskey please at $45.

A: Right, that will be one bottle of Johnnie Walker malt whiskey. <u>Is there anything else</u> you'd like sir?

B: Yes, I'd like these Ray Ban sunglasses.

A: They are priced at 170 US dollars. <u>Will that be all</u> sir?

B: Yes, That's everything Thanks.

A: The <u>total bill comes to</u> two hundred fifteen US dollars. Can I have your credit card please.

B: Sure, here you go.

A: Thank you. Please wait while I collect you duty-free goods.

B: Thank you.

Duty free: There are certain shops at international terminals which are free from taxes (duties)

Landing

"Ladies and gentlemen, American airline welcomes you to New York.

The local time is 11:25AM. For your safety please remain seated with your seat belt fastened and keep the aisle(s) clear until we are parked at the gate. The Captain will then turn off the "Fasten Seat Belt" sign, indicating it is safe to stand. Please use caution when opening the overhead compartments and removing items, since articles may have shifted during flight."

 Dialogue 1

A: Excuse me, sir. We'll be <u>landing</u> shortly. Would you please return your seat?

B: Oh I see. What is the <u>estimated time of arrival</u> in San Francisco?

A: 11:00 in the morning, local time. Please keep your seat belt fastened during the flight.

B: Thank you.

A: Thank you, Sir.

Landing: Plane down to the ground

emergency landing,

Cf) Take - off

ETA: Estimated time of arrival.

ETD: Estimated time of departure.

Cf) Actual flying time, Local time

Dialogue 2

A: What's the <u>time difference</u> between Incheon and London?

B: 8 hours.

A: What's the local time in London now?

B: Well, it's three in the morning.

A: Thank you.

B: <u>Don't mention it.</u>

Thank you!
- You're (very, more than, most) welcome.
- Not at all.
- Don't mention it.
- No worries.
- No problem.
- Sure.
- My pleasure.
- No, Thank YOU!

UNIT 5

Passport Control and Customs

Q 1. Can I see your passport?

Q 2. Are you a tourist or here on business?

    – Asked at customs to determine the <u>purpose of your visit</u>.

Q 3. Do you have anything to <u>declare</u>?

    – sometimes people need to declare things they bought in other countries.

Q 4. Have you brought any food into the country?

    – some countries do not allow certain foods to be brought into the country.

What's the purpose of your visit?

- I'm on vacation/ holiday.

- For my business

- Traveling

'Nothing to declare': It means that you are not bringing any goods that import duty.

Cf) Do you have anything to declare?

Dialogue 1

A: Good morning. May I see your passport?

B: Here you are.

A: Thank you very much. Are you a tourist or here on business?

B: I'm a tourist.

A: That's fine. Have a pleasant stay.

B: Thank you.

[Airport immigration questions]

Where have you flown from?
- I've flown from Incheon.

Where are you staying?
- Address of where you're staying.
- I'll will stay at Hilton Hotel.

What's the purpose of your visit?
- I'm travelling.
- I'm here for a business meeting.

How long will you be staying here?
- one week.

What's your occupation?
- Student, office worker, etc.

Dialogue 2

A: Good morning. Do you have anything to declare?

B: I'm not sure. I have two bottles of whiskey. Do I need to declare that?

A: No, you can have up to 2 <u>quarts</u>.

B: Great.

A: Have you brought any food into the country?

B: Just some cheese I bought in France.

A: <u>I'm afraid</u> I'll have to take that.

B: Why? It's just some cheese.

A: Unfortunately you are not allowed to bring cheese into the country.

B: OK. Here you are.

A: Thank you. Anything else?

B: I bought a T-shirt for my daughter.

A: That's fine. Have a nice day.

B: You, too.

Quart: 0.95 liter.
I'm afraid: polite way of telling unpleasant or disappointing.
      I'm afraid we can't come.
Allow: permit

Dialogue 3

A: Do you have anything to declare?

B: No, Nothing.

A: Could you open your bag please?

B: Certainly.

A: Do you bring any food or something?

B: No, I don't bring any food but I have some gifts for my son.

A: Ok, close your bag and give me a <u>customs declaration form</u> please.

B: Here you go.

A: Thank you. Have a great trip.

Customs: collects taxes on goods brought into the country.

Customs declaration form.

Customs office.

Customs officer.

TRAVELER DECLARATION FORM

- All arriving travelers must complete and submit this Customs Declaration form in accordance with the Customs Act and have personal effects inspected when designated by a customs officer.
- One form can be used for a family traveling together.
- Read "Attention" on the back before filling out this form.

Name			
Date of Birth		Passport Number	
Occupation		Length of Stay	days
Purpose of visit	☐ Sightseeing ☐ Government affairs	☐ Business ☐ Other	☐ Visiting friend
Flight No.		Accompany the size of a family	

Coumtries visited on this trip prior to entry to Korea (_____ countries total)

1.　　　　　　　　　　　2.　　　　　　　　　　　3.

Address in Korea	
Phone number (mobile)	☎ 　　　　　　　　(　　　　　　　　　　　)

GOODS SUBJECT TO DECLARATION
- Check ("√") the appropriate box below -

	YES	NO
1. Are you carrying any goods acguired (including purchase, donation, gift) from overseas (induding at domestic and foreign duty-free shops) that exceed duty-free allowance? (Refer to No. 1 on reverse.) [Total amount: approx.　　　　　　　　　　　] ※ If you voluntarily declare goods exceeding the duty-free allowance, the customs duties will be reduced by 30% (up to KRW 150,000).	☐	☐
2. Are you carrying any goods subject to preferential tariff treatment as originating in the country to which you have travelled?	☐	☐
3. Are you carrying any monetary instruments (Korean and foreign currencies, cashier's checks, other securities) valued more than US$ 10,000? [Total amount: approx.　　　　　　　　　　　]	☐	☐
4. Are you carrying any goods prohibited or restricted from entry into Korea such as firearms, knives, narcotics, artides in contravention to the national constitution, public security or morals? (Refer to No. 2 on reverse.)	☐	☐
5. Are you carrying any goods subject to quarantine such as animals, plants (fruits, seeds, saplings, etc.), livestock products (ham, beef jerky, roe, etc), or have you visited a farm in a country where a livestock epidemic disease has broken out? ※ Travelers who visited a farm in a country where a livestock epidemic disease has broken out must report to the Animal and Plant Quarantine Agency.	☐	☐
6. Are you carrying any commercial goods for sale, company goods (samples, etc), goods which you are custody and for taking out on departure?	☐	☐

I hereby dedare that the above statements are true to the best of my knowledge.

YY　　MM　　DD

Traveler's sionature.

[GOODS SUBJECT TO DECLARATION IN DETAIL]

► **Alcohol, cigarettes, perfume** (Report the entire amount for entry only if the duty-free allowance is exceeded)

Alcohol	( ) bottles. total ( )l. Value US$ ( )		
Cigarettes	( ) packs (20 pieces per pack)	Perfume	( )ml

► Other goods exceeding the duty-free allowance (US$ 600)

Item	Quantity / weight	Amount

1. DUTY-FREE ALLOWANCE

► **Alcohol, cigarettes, perfume (Applied separately to each item)**

Alcohol	Clgarette	Perfume
1 bottle (No more than 1l and valued less than US$ 400)	**200** pieces	**60**ml

► Passengers aged under 19 are not eligible for duty-free allowance regarding alcohol and cigarettes.
► **Other goods (Applied to combined value)**

Less than US$600 (Goods for personal use and gifts only)
* For agricultural/forestry/livestock products and Oriental medicinal herbs, the total value must not exceed KRW 100,000 and item-specific quantity or weight limits are applied.

2. GOODS PROHIBITED OR RESTRICTED FOR ENTRY INTO KOREA
• Firearms (gun replicas), knives, or other weapons, bullets and explosives, radioactive substances, monitoring instruments, etc.
• Methamphetamine, opium, heroin, cannabis and illicit drugs and abused/misused drugs
• Articles harmful to the national constitution, public security or morals or that divulge government secrets
• Fake goods or other items that infringe Intellectual Property Rights or counterfeit currency, notes or securities.
• Internationally protected endangered animals, plants, or products made from such (tigers, cobras, turtles, crocodile skin)

3. GOODS SUBJECT TO QUARANTINE
• Live animals (pets, etc), aquatic animals (fish, etc.), and livestock products (edible meat, beef jerky, sundae, sausages, ham, cheese, roe, etc.)
• Soil, fruits (mangoes, limes, apples, etc.), vegetables (chili, etc.), nuts (walnuts, etc.), seeds, and saplings, etc.
* **Fine may be imposed by law if not declared.**

※ ATTENTION
− Name should be identical with the Korean or English name printed on your passport.
− If you fail to dedare any goods subject to dedaration, declare goods falsely, or bring in goods via another person, you will be legally prosecuted, induding imprisonment for no more than 5 years, detention, an additional tax of 40% (60% if in violation more than twice within 2 years), noticed disposition, or confiscation of the goods in accordance with the Customs Act..
− Items meeting certain requirements under the FTA are eligible for preferential tariff treatment. In order to apply for preferential tariff treatment ex post facto, a general import declaration is required.
− If you have any questions, contact al customs officer or call 125.

NEW ZEALAND PASSENGER ARRIVAL CARD

APR 2022

- **This Arrival Card is a legal document – false declarations can lead to penalties including confiscation of goods, fines, prosecution, imprisonment, and deportation from New Zealand.**
- A separate Arrival Card must be completed for each passenger, including children.
- Please answer in English and fill in BOTH sides.
- Print in capital letters like this: NEW ZEALAND or mark answers like this:

1 Flight number/name of ship   Aircraft seat number

Overseas port where you boarded THIS aircraft/ship

Passport number

Nationality as shown on passport

Family name

Given or first names

Date of birth   day   month   year

Country of birth

Occupation or job

Full contact or residential
address in New Zealand

Email

Mobile/phone number

2a	**Answer this section if you live in New Zealand. Otherwise go to 2b.**

Which country did you spend most time in while overseas?

What was the MAIN reason for your trip?

- visiting friends/relatives
- business
- holiday/vacation
- conference/convention
- education
- other

Which country will you mostly live in for the next 12 months?   New Zealand   other

2b	**Answer this section if you DO NOT live in New Zealand.**

How long do you intend to stay in New Zealand?   Permanently   or   years   months   days

If you are not staying permanently what is your MAIN reason for coming to New Zealand?

- visiting friends/relatives
- business
- holiday/vacation
- conference/convention
- education
- other

In which country did you last live for 12 months or more?

State, province or prefecture   Zip or postal code

220401

3   List the countries you have been in during the past 30 days:

4	Do you know the contents of your baggage?	Yes	No

5 **Are you bringing into New Zealand:**

• **Any food:** cooked, uncooked, fresh, preserved, packaged or dried?	Yes	No
• **Animals or animal products:** including meat, dairy products, fish, honey, bee products, eggs, feathers, shells, raw wool, skins, bones or insects?	Yes	No
• **Plants or plant products:** fruit, flowers, seeds, bulbs, wood, bark, leaves, nuts, vegetables, parts of plants, fungi, cane, bamboo or straw, including for religious offerings or medicinal use?	Yes	No

Other biosecurity risk items, including:

• Animal medicines, biological cultures, organisms, soil or water?	Yes	No
• Equipment/clothing used with animals, plants or water, including for gardening, beekeeping, fishing, water sport or diving activities?	Yes	No
• Items that have been used for outdoor activities, including any footwear, tents, camping, hunting, hiking, golf or sports equipment?	Yes	No
In the past 30 days (while outside New Zealand) have you visited any wilderness areas, had contact with animals (except domestic cats and dogs) or visited properties that farm or process animals or plants?	Yes	No

WARNING: false declaration can incur $400 INSTANT FINE

6 **Are you bringing into New Zealand:**

• **Medicine:** over 3 months' supply, or medicine not prescribed to you?	Yes	No
• **Restricted or prohibited goods:** for example, weapons, indecent publications, endangered plants or wildlife, illegal or controlled drugs?	Yes	No
• **Alcohol:** more than 3 bottles of spirits (not exceeding 1.125 litres each) and 4.5 litres of wine or beer?	Yes	No
• **Tobacco:** more than 50 cigarettes or 50 grams of tobacco products (including a mixture of cigarettes and other tobacco products)?	Yes	No
• **Goods obtained overseas and/or purchased duty-free in New Zealand:** with a total value of more than NZ$700 (including gifts)?	Yes	No
• **Goods carried for business or commercial use?**	Yes	No
• **Goods carried on behalf of another person?**	Yes	No
• **Cash:** NZ$10,000 or more (or foreign equivalent), including travellers cheques, bank drafts, money orders, etc?	Yes	No

WARNING: false declaration can incur $400 INSTANT FINE

7

Do you hold a current New Zealand passport, a residence class visa or a returning resident's visa? If yes, go to **10**.	Yes	No
Are you a New Zealand citizen using a foreign passport? If yes, go to **10**.	Yes	No
Do you hold an Australian passport, Australian Permanent Residence Visa or Australian Resident Return Visa? – If yes go to **9**	Yes	No

8 **All others.**
You must leave New Zealand before expiry of your visa or face deportation.

Are you coming to New Zealand for medical treatment or consultation
or to give birth?   Yes   No

Select one I hold a temporary entry class visa (Tick yes if you currently
             hold a visa, even if it is not attached as a label to your passport).   Yes

        or I do not hold a visa and am applying for a visitor visa on arrival.   Yes

9 Have you ever been sentenced to 12 months or more in prison, or
been deported, removed or excluded from any country at any time?   Yes   No

10 **I declare that the information I have given is true, correct, and complete.**

Signature   Date

(parent or guardian must sign for children under the age of 18)

The Privacy Act 2020 provides rights of access to, and correction of, personal information.
If you wish to exercise these rights please contact the New Zealand Customs Service on
0800 428 786 or Email: feedback@customs.govt.nz and/or Immigration New Zealand at
PO Box 1473, Wellington.

UNIT 6

Meeting at the airport

Dialogue 1

A: Where will you meet your father?

B: I'll meet him at arrival gate 2.

A: When will he get there?

B: <u>I have no idea</u>.

Dialogue 2

A: What time are you meeting your friends?

B: I'm meeting them at nine o'clock tonight.

A: How are they getting here?

B: They are <u>coming by</u> taxi.

Dialogue 3

A: Is this American Airlines?

B: Yes, how can I help you?

A: Could you tell me when flight AA123 will arrive?

B: Wait a second, please. I'll check.

I have no idea = I don't know

Ex) I have no idea him (X) / I don't know him (O)

I have no idea where she is. (O) / I don't know where she is. (O)

I have no idea what to do / I have no idea what happened.

Dialogue 4

A: All the arriving flights are listed on that board?

B: Yes, do you need help?

A: Do they have an arrival gate listed?

B: No, they'll probably list it about twenty minutes before arrival.

UNIT 7

Tourist information center at the airport

 Dialogue 1

A: <u>I was wondering if</u> you could help me book a few tours.

B: You have come to the right place.

How long will you be here?

A: I'm staying for one week.

B: Have you ever visited this city before?

A: No, this is my first time visiting here.

B: What are you interested in?

Do you enjoy museums and buildings, or would you rather visit our

magnificent amusement park?

A: I really enjoy visiting museums and art galleries.

B: We have tours for all interests.

A: Do you have a city tour?

B: Yes, in fact, I usually suggest that to visitors.

A general city tour is an excellent tour to start with.

I was wondering if···.

Ex) I was wondering if I could ask you a few questions.

I was wondering if I could borrow your money.

Dialogue 2

A: Hello, you could tell me how can I get to the Maple Hotel from here?

B: Yes, you can take the subway yellow line at the airport station.

A: How long does it take to get there?

B: It's about 40 minutes.

A: Thank you very much.

B: Have a nice trip.

Dialogue 3

A: How can I help you?

B: Hello! I have a few questions.

A: OK, go ahead.

B: Do you have any brochures or some book for this city?

A: Well, we have a few interesting tour guide books here.

B: That sounds great. Could you recommend a good place to visit?

A: Let's see. There is an 19 th century palace. It's 15 minutes away from here. You can find the directions and tips in this book.

B: That's wonderful. I'll go there. Thank you very much.

A: You're welcome, have a good day!

Dialogue 4

A: Hello!

B: Hi How can I help you?

A: I'd like to know where I can try local cuisine.

B: Here! Take these pamphlets. Here are the names and addresses of quite a few restaurants that serve great local cuisine. Look, they even have maps with directions on the back.

(The clerk shows a map on one of the pamphlets)

B: You are here right now. This is where the closest restaurant is. Will you be able to find your way?

A: Yes, thank you. And I have another question, if you don't mind.

B: Not at all! What else would you like to know?

A: Where can I find information on local events?

B: There will be a beer festival next week, so you can visit it or information about events in neighboring towns you can read this!

A: Thank you very much!

B: It was a pleasure, Have a nice day!

CHAPTER

3

Hotel

CHAPTER
3   Hotel

UNIT 1

Hotel Reservation

Useful expressions 1 (receptionist)

1. Royal Hotels, Amy speaking. How can I help you?

2. What date are you looking for?

3. How long will you be staying?

4. How many adults will be in the room?

5. How many people are there in your party?

6. I'm afraid we are fully booked.

7. There are only a few vacancies left.

8. We advise that you book in advance during peak season.

9. Do you want a smoking or non-smoking room?

10. The breakfast is open from 6am until 10 am.

11. We have an indoor swimming pool and sauna.

12. We serve a continental breakfast.

13. Cable television is included, but the movie channel is extra.

14. How would you like to pay sir?

15. The rate I can give you is 99.54 with tax.

16. We require a credit card number for a deposit.

Useful expression 2 (Guest)

1. I'd like to make a reservation.

2. I'd like a room for 3 nights, please?

3. Do you have any rooms available for the day after tomorrow?

4. Breakfast included?

5. Can I see the room, Please?

6. Do you have a room with a bath?

7. What time is breakfast and where is the restaurant?

8. I'll arrive on tomorrow night.

9. I'm going to stay for 3nights.

10. Are there any laundry facilities?

11. I'd like to change my room because the room is too noisy.

12. Can I have another room please, this one is very small.

13. My room's not been made up. Please make up my room.

14. I've lost my room key.

15. The key doesn't work.

16. Is there an airport shuttle bus?

17. Could I have a wake-up call at 6 o'clock please?

18. We're checking out now.

19. Could you call me a tax?

Dialogue 1

A: Good morning, Double Tree hotel. How can I help you?

B: Hello, I'd like to <u>make a reservation</u> a room for tonight.

A: What kind of room would you like?

B: I would like a double room, please.

A: Hold on please, I'll check. I'm afraid we only have twin room available tonight. But tomorrow we will have a double room.

B: OK, that will do. How much for a twin room?

A: 120 dollars including tax.

B: Are meals included in that price?

A: Yes, only breakfast is included.

B: That's wonderful, I will take a twin room for tonight and change to a double room tomorrow.

A: Ok. thank you.

Make a reservation: reserve, book.

Ex) I'd like to make a reservation a room.

I'd like to reserve a room.

I'd like to book a room.

Dialogue 2

A: Hello, welcome to Waterfront Hotel. How can I help you?

B: Hello, I would like a room for tonight. Do you have any <u>vacancies</u>?

A: Yes sir, would you like a single room, or a double room?

B: A single room, please.

A: How long will you be staying?

B: For two nights.

A: Okay, would you like a king size bed or a queen size?

B: Well, queen size bed, please.

A: Sure, and would you rather have a room with a view of the ocean or the forest?

B: It doesn't really matter to me, whichever one is cheaper.

A: Sure, it's going to be $65 per night. Can I have your ID, please?

B: Here it is.

A: Alright, Could you sign here, please?

B: No problem. Do you accept Visa card?

A: Sure, any Visa, Master Card or American Express.

B: Perfect, here is my card.

A: Thank you. Is there a phone number where you can be contacted?

B: Yes, it is 135-6749.

A: Okay. Here's your key. Your room number is 358. It's on the 3rd floor, you can take the elevators behind us. If you need anything, just dial 9 for the reception.

B: Thank you for your help.

A: My pleasure. Enjoy your stay!

Dialogue 3

A: Hello, Hilton hotel, how may I help you?

B: Yes, I'd like to book a room for tomorrow.

A: Certainly, what kind of room would you like?

B: single room please.

A: when will you be leaving?

B: July, 15th.

A: Ok, may I have your name and phone number please?

B: Gunn, That's G-U-N-N. and 010-125-4596.

A: Thank you. Have a nice day.

B: Thank you. Bye.

Vacancy: a room that is available in a hotel, etc.

   Ex) I'm sorry, we have no vacancies.

Room types

   Single room- single bed for one person.

   Double room – One double bed for two people.

   Twin room - Two single bed for two people.

   Triple room – Three single bed or one double bed + one single bed.

   Suite room – a set of rooms.

Hotel Reservation Request Form

Full Name		
	First Name	Last Name
Address		
Phone Number		
E-mail		
Arrival Date and Time	MM-DD-YYYY	HH:MM
Departure Date and Time	MM-DD-YYYY	HH:MM
Number of Adults		Number of Kids	
Payment Method	○ Credit card　　　○ Cash　　　○ Wire	
Do you have any special request		

UNIT 2

Check in Hotel

 Dialogue 1

A: I'd like a room for two people, for two nights please.

B: Ok, fill out this form please. Do you need breakfast?

A: Yes.

B: Breakfast starts from 6 to 10 am in the dining room on the first floor. Here is your key. Your room number is 212 on the second floor. Enjoy your stay.

A: Thank you.

Dialogue 2

A: Hello, how can I help you.

B: I'd like a single room please.

A: Do you have a reservation?

B: No. I don't.

A: How many nights?

B: Just one night, please.

A: Do you want breakfast?

B: No, I don't need breakfast.

A: Ok, That'll be $100. Do you want to pay now or when you check out?

B: I'd like to pay now.

A: Please fill this out and sign here please.

B: Ok A: Can I see your ID?

B: Here is my passport.

A: Thank you, here is your receipt and your key.

B: Thank you.

UNIT 3

Doorperson and Bellboy

 Dialogue 1

A: Good morning sir. Do you have any luggage with you?

B: Yes, in the trunk.

A: I'd check your luggage. I have two pieces of luggage, is that correct?

B: Yes, that's right.

A: Follow me to the lobby please.

B: Sure, Thank you.

A: <u>Mind your step</u>, please.

Mind your step! : watch your step!

B: Thank you.

A: You're welcome.

Dialogue 2

A: Can I help you with your baggage?

B: That's Ok, It's not heavy. I can take care of it. thank you.

A: You can check -in at the front desk right over there.

B: Thank you.

A: Please be careful of using <u>revolving door</u>. It's automatic.

B: Thank you so much.

Revolving: turn in a circle

Ex) Revolving door, revolving chair, revolving stage. revolver.

Dialogue 3

A: Are you ready to go to your room now Ms. Louis?

B: Certainly,

A: Ms. Louis, this is your room. I'll check your room first. This is luggage rack; the television has 40 channels. If you'd like to make a call outside press No 1. Information 2. Restaurant 3. housekeeping 4. Front desk 0. And if you need me to help you, you can call <u>concierge</u> and press number 7. Do you follow me Ms. Louis?

B: Yes.

A: Any other questions?

B: No, thank you.

A: You're welcome. Enjoy your stay.

B: Thank you.

Concierge: to help guests by giving them information, arranging something etc.

Dialogue 4

A: "Excuse me Mr. Cruise. For your information, our restaurant is located on the second floor next to the Bar. It is open start from 06:30 to 22:00. We serve a buffet breakfast from 06:30 AM to 11.00 AM. We have a gym as well. The gym located on the ground floor behind the lobby and business center also in the same floor, beside the gym. If you want to do workout, you will able to use our gym free of charge from 06:00 to 22:00."

B: "Lovely ···"

UNIT
4

Telephone Operator

Dialogue 1

A: Hello This is operator. How may I help you?

B: Yes, could you give me a wake-up call at 6 am.?

A: Ok, May I have your name and room number please?

B: This is Tom cruise in room 247.

A: Alright, Mr. Cruise in room 247, wake-up call at 6 am.

B: Thank you.

Dialogue 2

A: Good morning, this is operator. May I help you.

B: Good morning, could you get me 325-3468, please.

A: Yes, hold the line please… I'm sorry but your party doesn't answer.

B: Ok, Thank you. I'll try next time.

Telephone Expressions

1. John speaking. What can I do for you?
2. Who's calling please?
3. Thank you for calling.
4. Can I talk to Mr. Denial?
5. Just a second, I'll get her.
6. Hang on a second. I'll check if he is in.
7. Please hold on while I put you through to the office.
8. Could you please repeat that?
9. Could you speak up a little?
10. Could you speak a little slower please?
11. Please let me know when he'll be in home.
12. Can I call you again? I think we have a bad connection.
13. I have another call. Please hold on a second.
14. Can I take a message?
15. Would you like to leave a message?
16. I'm sorry, but He is not here at the moment. Could you leave a message?
17. She just stepped out at the moment. Can she call you back when she is back?
18. Fine. I'll let him know you called.

Dialogue 3

A: Good afternoon, Ann speaking. How can I help you?

B: Hello, can you put me through to room 101 please?

A: Hold on please⋯ I'm sorry, there is no answer the phone.

B: Ok, I'll try again later. Thank you.

A: Thank you.

UNIT 5

Room Service

Dialogue 1

A: Good evening, Room service. Can I help you?

B: Yes, I want my breakfast in my room tomorrow.

A: What would you like to have?

B: I'll have some toast, boiled eggs, and coffee please

A: What time would you like it served?

B: At six O'clock, please.

A: Alright, Sir.

B: Thank you.

Dialogue 2

A: Good morning, May I help you?

B: Yes, I'd like to have breakfast in my room.

A: Ok, Can I take your order now?

B: Please bring me some hot cake, apple juice, eggs, and coffee.

A: How would you like your eggs?

B: Sunny-side up please.

A: What time do you want sir?

B: At seven please.

A: May I have your name and room number, please?

UNIT 6

Housekeeping

 Dialogue 1

A: Good morning?

Are you from <u>housekeeping</u>.

B: Yes, how can I help you?

A: It seems that you <u>are about to</u> service our room.

B: Yes, Madam, that's right.

I am going to service your room next.

A: Could you do it a little late, please. My daughter is still sleeping.

So I don't want to wake her up right now.

B: Certainly, just put the DND (<u>Do Not Disturb</u>) sign on the door.

A: That's great. I will put it on right now.

   Thank you.

B: You're welcome.

Housekeeping: That is responsible for cleaning the hotel room.

   Ex) Call housekeeping and ask them to bring us some clean towels.

Be about to: be going to.

   Ex) She is about to cry.

   I'm about to study.

   I'm about to call you.

Do Not Disturb - a sign placed on the outside of the door of a hotel room.

UNIT 7

Laundry service

Dialogue 1

A: Hello. Could you please send someone to <u>pick up</u> my laundry from my room?

B: Sure, would you want me to send the staff right now or later?

A: I'm leaving in about twenty minutes.

So If you could send the staff right now, that would be great.

B: Sure, that won't be a problem.

What is your room number by the way?

A: My room number is 256.

When will the clothes be returned to my room?

B: Well, <u>it usually takes</u> a day so should be ready to collect tomorrow evening, but you can ask the laundry staff for a better <u>estimate</u>.

A: Alright, Thank you.

Pick up: select, gather, harvest, choose.

Pick up the ball!

I'll pick you up at five.

The phone rang and rang and nobody picked up.

It takes about 10 minutes.

Estimate: calculate roughly, guess··· How much do you estimate?

Estimate arrival time / Estimate departure time

Dialogue 2

A: This is laundry service Can I help you?

B: I have several clothes that need to be washed.

   Some t-shirts, and one sweatshirts.

A: Will that be all?

B: Oh, I forgot. I also have a sweater that need to be dry cleaned.

A: OK, what is your room number?

B: 321

A: Please fill out the laundry request form and place your laundry in the

   laundry bag.

B: Alright. Thank you.

Useful words of laundry

Fabric softener / Washing powder / soap / laundry bag / Laundry basket / Clothes hanger / Clothes peg / Washing machine / hand wash / Iron / Ironing board / Tumble dryer / Detergent / Bleaching / Laundromat / Stain.

UNIT 8

At the Bar

 Dialogue 1

A: Good evening, sir. What can I get for you?

B: A bottle of beer, Please. What would you like, Lina?

C: A vodka and tonic, please.

A: Would you like ice and lemon in that, Madam?

C: Yes, please.

A: Shall I <u>charge</u> this to your room?

B: Yes, Please.

A: May I have your Key card, Please?

B: Here you go.

A: That's 25 Dollars. Sign here please.

Dialogue 2

A: Hello, what can I get you?

B: I'd like beer please.

A: Would you like <u>draft</u> or bottled beer?

B: Bottled, please.

Charge: fee, fare, rate, service charge

Draft beer: beer on tap.

Dialogue 3

A: Here you go, a large whisky and a dry martini.

Shall I charge it to your room?

B: No, I'll pay by cash now. How much is that?

A: That comes to 18 dollars plus tax.

B: Ok. Keep the change.

A: Thank you sir.

 Dialogue 4

A: Good evening, what can I get for you?

B: May I see the wine menu?

A: Certainly, here it is.

B: Thanks.

A: Have you decided?

B: I think so. Do these come by the glass?

A: Yes, of cause.

B: Ok. I'll have a glass of Pinot Noir. please.

A: Sure, I'll bring it right to you.

B: Thank you.

A: Would you like to charge this to your room?

B: Yes, please charge my drink to my room now.

A: very good.

Useful expressions at the bar

What can I get for you? What can I get you?

Do you want a pint or a glass? (a Pint=20 oz, a glass=sleeve=12 oz)

Do you want a double?

On the rocks please.

Do you have a designated driver?

Could you call me a taxi, please?

What do you have on tap?

Do you have anything local beer? (domestic beer, imported beer)

I'll have a glass of wine.

It's on me.

I'll buy the next round.

It's on the house.

Happy hour: A time of the day at the bar when drink and food are discounted (3pm-6pm)

Top shelf liquor: Ex) 'My rich friend only drink top-shelf liquor'

Hard liquor: strong alcohol like vodka.

Booze: alcohol

Alcohol beverage / Non-alcohol beverage / Soft drink / Soda

Bouncer: security guard at the bar.

About Tip

: You don't need to say anything when you leave a tip to a bartender.

You can just leave the money on the bar or table. Sometimes there is a cup marked "Tips" to put money in. A tip is usually about 15-20% of the price of the drink or bill.

You can say 'That's for you'.

UNIT 9

Breakfast

 Dialogue 1

A: Good morning? Sir. may I see your room number.

B: Good morning? My room number is 123.

Can I have <u>a table for two</u> please.

A: Ok, come this way please.

B: Thank you.

A: This is buffet style. Would you like coffee?

B: Yes, please.

Dialogue 2

A: Good morning. Are you ready to order?

B: Yes, I'll have two scrambled eggs and cereal with milk please.

A: Anything to drink?

B: Tomato juice and coffee please.

A: Anything else?

B: Could I have a slice of cheese?

A: Sure, coming right up.

I'd like a table for four.

I want a table for one.

Dialogue 3

A: Good morning? Are you ready to order?

B: Yes, eggs and pancakes please.

A: How would you like your eggs?

B: Sunny-side up please.

A: Very good, care for some coffee?

B: Yes, Make it <u>decaf</u> please?

Decaf: decaffeinated coffee.

American breakfast: not too light and not too heavy. Coffee is the most preferred beverage. Chilled water is served before breakfast.

Menu: Fruit juice/ Fresh fruits/ breakfast cereals/ Eggs to order / Ham, steak, sausages/ Grilled tomatoes/ mushroom/ potatoes/ Pancakes/ waffles with syrup and honey/ Breakfast rolls/ bread/ toast/ Muffins/ better/ preserves/ coffee/tea.

Continental breakfast: is very light morning breakfast. usually served in a buffet and is also designed by European breakfast.

How to cook eggs

Sunny Side Up: it is cooked until the whites are solid but the yolk is still runny, Round yellow yolk gives a sun-like appearance.

Over Easy: Cooked on both sides, but the yolk remains runny.

Over Hard: Cooked on both sides until the yolk is fully cooked.

Poached: Cooked outside the shell in boiling water until the whites are hard and the yolk is still runny.

Hard Boiled: boiled in their shells in water until the yolks are fully cooked.

Soft Boiled: cooked in their shells in water until the yolk is jammy.

Scrambled: Scrambled eggs are beaten and then gently cooked, scraping them into folds.

UNIT 10

Dinner

 Dialogue 1

A: Hello! how can I help you?

B: Hello! I would like a table for one please.

A: Of cause, please follow me.

Here is a table for one.

B: Thank you. Could you give us the menu, please?

A: Yes, Of course. Here you are.

B: Thank you.

A: Can I get you anything to drink?

B: Just water for me.

A: Great! I'll be right back.

(a few min. later...)

A: Are you ready to order?

B: Yes, I'll have the grilled Salmon and Salad.

A: Would you like a starter. Sir?

B: Yes, I'd like the mushroom soup.

A: Excellent, I'll be right back.

(after the meal)

A: Did you enjoy your meal?

B: Yes, it was wonderful. Thank you.

A: Would you like something for dessert?

B: Yes, for dessert, I'll have Ice cream please.

(after the dessert)

B: Excuse me.

A: Yes, sir How can I help you?

B: Could you bring me a glass of water, please?

A: Yes, Of course.

B: Thank you.

A: Can I bring anything else?

B: No, thank you. just the bill.

A: Ok sir, I'll be right back with the bill.

How to have good table manners

1. Wash your hands before you sit down.

2. Put your phone on silent.

3. Wait for everyone to be seated.

4. Place your napkin on your lap.

5. Pass all food dishes to the right.

6. Don't eat until the host eats.

7. Use the utensils from the outside in.

8. Keep your elbows off the table.

9. Eat slowly and with your mouth closed.

10. Say 'please' and 'thank you.'

11. Take part in the conversation.

12. Cover your mouth if you need to burp.

13. Pick up your utensils if you drop down.

14. Instead of reaching across the table for something, ask for it to be passed to you.

15. Put your utensils on your plate when you're done.

Dialogue 2

A: Hi How are you doing?

B: Fine, Thank you. Can I see a menu, please?

A: Certainly, here it is.

B: Thank you, What's today's special?

A: Grilled pork and cheese on salad.

B: That sound great. I'll try that.

A: Would you like something to drink?

B: Yes, I would like a coke, Please.

A: I'll be right back.

B: Thanks.

Dialogue 3

A: Can I get you anything else?

B: No thanks. I'd like the check, Please.

A: It comes to $25.98.

B: Here you are. Keep the change!

A: Thank you, Have a great day!

Asking and ordering food

Good evening. I'd like a table for 3.

Could we have a <u>table in the corner</u>?

               table by the window?

               table outside?

               table on the terrace?

Where are the restroom?

Can you serve me right away? I'm in a hurry.

What's the price of the fixed menu?

Is service included?

Could we have <u>a bottle of beer</u> please?

               Another chair

               Chopsticks

               Fork and knife

               Glass of water

               Napkin/ Plate / Spoon / Toothpick

UNIT 11

Swimming pool

Dialogue 1

A: Excuse me, is there a swimming pool in this hotel?

B: Sorry, we don't have a full-sized one, but we do have <u>individual</u> swim stations.

A: That sounds good, is there an <u>extra charge</u> for these swim station?

B: If you're a <u>registered</u> guest, you have free <u>access</u> to our swim stations.

A: Excellent, now what are the hours?

B: They open from 7am to 10pm.

A: Thank you.

Individual: Each, Personal, Private. Single member of a group

Extra charge:

    ex) Breakfast is provided at no extra charge.

Register: Put name on list

Access: approach, enter,

    Ex) High-speed internet access.

      You need a password to get access to the computer.

UNIT 12

Fitness center

  Dialogue 1

A: Excuse me. Does this hotel have a <u>fitness center</u>?

B: Yes, we have a <u>gym</u>.

A: Where is the gym located?

B: The gym <u>is located in</u> 2nd floor. Take the elevator or the stairs. You can't miss it.

A: Is there any <u>additional surcharge</u> for the gym?

B: No, the gym is free to our guests. Just bring your room key.

A: Ok, what time is the gym open and does it close?

B: It opens <u>twenty-four hours a day, seven days a week</u>.

A: That's wonderful.

Fitness: physical exercise, fitness training, fitness trainer,

Gym: gymnasium, fitness center,

     Ex) I work out at the gym most days. (*work out = exercise)

Be located in: be situated, lie in

     Ex) Hanok village is located in Jeonju.

Surcharge: extra charge.

Twenty-four hours a day and seven days a week = 24/7 = every day.

UNIT 13

Money exchange

 Dialogue 1

A: Excuse me, I'd like to <u>exchange</u> some money.

B: Ok, could you fill out this form. please?

A: Ok. Here you are.

B: So, you want to change Dollars to Won, is that correct?

A: Yes, That's right.

B: Can I see your passport?

A: Here you are.

B: You want to exchange 500USD to Won.

The <u>current rate</u> is one dollar to 1000 Won.

So, that will be 500,000Won.

A: Ok, that's great.

B: Would you like that in small or large bills? Or mix of <u>both</u>?

A: I'd like a mix of both.

B: Ok, no problem. Please sign here.

And here are 6 - 50,000 won notes and 20 - 10,000won notes.

For a total of 500,000 won.

A: Thank you very much.

Exchange: money exchange, currency exchange.

Ex) Could you tell me where the money exchange is?

Current rate: cf) exchange rate. foreign exchange rate.

UNIT 14

Concierge

 Dialogue 1

A: How can I help you?

B: Could you <u>recommend</u> any good restaurants around here? I'd like to eat Italian food tonight.

A: There <u>a couple of</u> excellent Italian restaurants in the down town.

B: Ok good. How can I <u>get to</u> there? Can I walk?

A: You can walk, but it takes about 30 minutes. Or you can take the bus from the <u>bus stop</u> in front of the hotel. <u>Get off</u> at the central station.

B: Do buses regularly go to the down town?

A: Yes, it <u>runs</u> every 10 minutes until midnight.

B: Thank you.

Recommend: suggest, advise,

      Ex) I strongly(highly) recommend a Marriott hotel.

A couple of: about two.

      Ex) a couple of days ago / I will be there in a couple of minutes.

Get to: come to, reach, arrive

Bus stop: cf) Bus station, Bus terminal.

Run: cf) Buses to London run every half hour.

      He runs Korean restaurant.

UNIT 15

Check out

 Dialogue 1

A: Good morning, Can I help you?

B: Yes, I'd like to check out today.

A: May I ask your room number, please?

B: My room number is 743.

A: Ok, have you used any of our service?

B: Yes, I used laundry service.

A: Ok, here is you bill. you have been charged for 450 dollars including laundry service.

B: I guess everything is great. Can I pay by credit card?

A: Of course, May I see your card please?

B: Here you are.

A: Please sign your name here.

B: Sure.

A: Have a great day

B: You too.

Dialogue 2

A: Good morning. how can I help you?

B: Hi! I'm leaving now. Here is my room key.

A: Thank you. Please wait a second, I'll give you your <u>receipt</u>.

   Here you go.

B: Thank you

A: Did you enjoy your stay here?

B: Yes, I really had a great time in here.

A: Do you need a taxi or any help?

B: Yes, I need a taxi to go to the airport.

A: Ok, if you <u>step out</u> the front doors, the doorman will call a taxi for

   you. have a safe trip home.

B: Thank you.

Receipt: piece of paper showing what was paid for.

    Can I have a receipt, please?

    Give me the receipt, Please?

Step out: to go out.

    I need to step out for a moment.

UNIT 16

Hotel Manners and Etiquettes

For the guests

1. Try not to make unnecessary noise.

2. Be polite to the staff.

3. Always fill out the survey after your stay.

4. Respect the hotel property.

5. Hang up towels you don't need replaced.

6. Avoid pocketing too much food from breakfast.

7. Make it easy for the housekeeper to do their job.

8. Check in and out on time.

9. Tip where appropriate.

10. Respect elevator etiquette

11. Keep a close eye on your children.

12. Dress appropriately.

13. Avoid bringing home the hotel linens.

14. Show good manners to other guests.

For hotel staff

1. Always greet guest and colleagues with a smile and maintain a friendly and pleasant expression.

2. Stand upright, do not fold your arms in front of the guest.

3. Keep your hands out of your pockets.

4. Do not lean on the counter at any time and especially when dealing with the guest.

5. Ensure a positive body language at all times.

6. Always be courteous, never argue with guests.

7. Be humored and even-tempered, do not become over friendly with guests.

8. Always be attentive when speaking to guest and look at a guest when addressing him / her.

9. Always look and act professionally, do understand that there are other guests watching your behavior.

10. Always appear confident and be positive.

11. Always listen carefully to the guest when talking to him/ her.

12. Try to use the guest's name at least twice once known.

13. Try to ask the right questions to identify the needs of the guests.

14. Talk clearly and maintain a good tone of voice at all times.

15. Do not criticize one guest to another.

16. A Have a good knowledge of the place and surroundings where the hotel is situated, eg: nearby places of interest, distance to the airport etc.

17. Always give the guest a warm and friendly welcome.

18. Make the guest feel comfortable and safe.

29. Take your time for the guest and do not rush with them.

20. Always recommend in-house hotels services to the guest and provide with a brochure or additional details if required.

21. Have a good knowledge of the place and surroundings where the hotel is situated, eg: nearby places of interest, distance to the airport etc.

CHAPTER

4 Situational Conversation

CHAPTER
4 Situational Conversation

UNIT 1

Local Transportation

 Dialogue 1

Taxi

A: Hello, <u>Where to</u>. sir?

B: Hello, to the airport please.

A: Ok, do you need to put your bag in the <u>boot</u>?

B: No thanks, I'll carry it with me. How long does it take?

A: It's about 20minutes. Are you in a hurry?

B: Yes, I'm a bit late.

A: Ok, shall we take the expressway? There is an extra charge.

B: That's good, thanks.

A: Fasten your seatbelt, please.

B: Ok,

A: Now here is the expressway.

   Can I have 4 dollars for the charge?

B: Here you are.

A: Which terminal?

B: International terminal 1. please.

A: Ok, here is the terminal 1.

B: Thanks. How much is it?

A: 66 dollars.

B: Here is 70 dollars. Keep the change.

A: Thank you. have a good trip.

B: Ok. Have a good day!

Where to? = Where are you going?
Boot = Trunk

Useful expressions for taxi

Excuse me, could you hail a taxi for me please?

Could you take me to Jade Hotel?

How much is the fare?

Can I get a ride?

How long will it take?

Do you use a meter?

Please keep the meter running.

Do you have <u>flat rate (charge, fee, price)</u> to the hotel?

I'm in a rush(hurry)

Can you take the quickest route please?

Is it okay if I open a window?

Air-conditioning Please.

Can you get there by 11am?

Do you accept credit card?

Keep the change or Here's a tip.

Where are you going?

Where is your destination?

I don't have any change.

Do you have smaller bills?

There is a toll fee, you have to pay Ok?

There is a traffic jam.

It's rush hour.

Taxi stand.

Dialogue 2

Bus stop

A: Hi! is this the bus stop?

B: That's right. Is this your first time taking the bus?

A: Yes, I usually drive.

B: Which bus are you waiting for?

A: I'm not sure. I've been waiting here for half an hour.

I'm trying to get to town but I'm not sure what bus to take.

B: The bus Number 90 will take you to the town.

A: Do you know when the next bus will arrive?

B: They arrive every 10 minutes. Look there is the 90!

A: Thank you so much for your help.

Dialogue 3

Bus stop

A: Excuse me. Are you able to help me, please?

B: Sure. How can I help you?

A: I don't know how to get to the city hall by bus.

B: Yes, take the 124 bus. Blue one.

A: That's really helpful. Thank you.

Dialogue 4

Train station

A: I'd like a ticket to Interlaken please.

B: One way or round trip?

A: Round trip please.

B: That's €12.50. here is your ticket.

A: What platform is it?

B: Platform 3.

A: Thank you.

Dialogue 5

Train station

A: Hello. I'd like to <u>purchase</u> a ticket.

B: Where are you going?

A: I'm going to Lauterbrunnen.

B: How are you looking to travel? Economy or Business class?

A: What is the difference between the two?

B: Economy is a standard seat. There are four seats to a car.

Business class has <u>reclining</u> seats with two seats per car.

A: Is there Wi-Fi <u>available</u>?

B: Sure.

A: What is the price difference?

B: A one-way economy fare is $25. Business class is $50.

A: I'll take a one-way economy.

Purchase = buy

Reclining = lean, bend

Available = free, empty, vacant, unoccupied.

Dialogue 6

Subway station

A: Excuse me. Could you tell me how I can get a subway ticket?

B: You can use the auto ticket machine over there.

A: Oh I see. I'm a new here. Can you show me how to use it?

B: Sure. Put the money in the slot and click 'One ticket' button on the screen.

A: Ok, I think I can handle it. Thank you so much.

B: We're welcome.

Dialogue 7

Subway station

A: Can I have a ticket?

B: To which station?

A: I'm going to the national museum. Which line should I take?

B: Take the Line 3 and <u>transfer</u> to Line 2 at the City Hall.

A: Ok, how many stops in total?

B: 7 stops. This is the subway map.

A: Thank you. How much is the ticket?

B: $2.

I'm a new here = I'm a stranger here myself.

Slot = cf, Slot machine.

Transfer: Move from one place to another.

    Cf) money transfer / transfer student /

UNIT 2

At the cafe

Dialogue 1

A: Hello. I'd like a cup of coffee Please.

B: Which size?

A: A large cup.

B: Any particular favor?

A: Mocha latte please. Is whipped cream extra?

B: No, the same price. Is that all?

A: Yes, that's it. thanks

Dialogue 2

A: Hi, what can I get you?

B: I'd like a Frappuccino with whip please.

A: Did you say with or without whip?

B: With whip.

A: Got it. Which size?

B: Grande please.

A: What's your name?

B: Gunn.

A: That'll be $4.50.

B: Here you are. Thanks

A: Gunn! Here is your Frappuccino.

B: Thanks.

UNIT 3

Coffee

Affogato

a coffee based dessert where a scoop of ice cream or gelato.

Americano

a coffee beverage where a shot or two of espresso with hot water.

Barista

Person who prepares and serves coffee at a café

Black Eye Coffee

a cup of regular drip coffee with two shots of espresso pouring into it.

Cappuccino

a coffee drink which is served with three layers, first a shot of espresso, followed by a pour of steamed milk, and then a dollop of foamed.

Crema

the coffee oil that floats to the top of a coffee. It remains on a latte or other milk-based espresso.

Decaf Coffee

Decaffeinated coffee. Most or all of the caffeine has been removed.

Drip coffee

the coffee's flavor is extracted through contact with the water without pressure.

Espresso

made by forcing boiling water through grounded coffee beans, using pressure to extract the flavor from the coffee and into the water.

Espresso con panna

is espresso, either single shot or double shot, topped with whipped cream rather than regular milk.

Flat white

is an espresso where 'flat' steamed milk (without frothy foam) gets a shot of espresso.

Latte

a café latte is an espresso beverage where a shot or two of espresso gets added to steamed milk.

Long back

popular in New Zealand and Australia for a shot or two of espresso pouring into a mug of hot water.

Macchiato

is made with a shot of espresso and just a small amount of foamed milk.

Mocha

a café mocha, also known as a moccaccino, is a chocolate-flavored variation of a standard latte. Cocoa powder mixed into the latte with sugar.

Short black

similar to a café Americano

UNIT 4

Fast food restaurant

Dialogue 1

A: Excuse me. I'd like the combo set number 1. please.

B: What kind of drink would you like?

A: Sugar fee coke please.

B: Would you like a large coke for 50 cents more?

A: No thanks.

B: For here or to go?

A: To go.

B: Alright. That will be 9.50 dollars.

A: Here you go.

B: Thanks.

Dialogue 2

A: Hello, I want 6 chicken nuggets please.

B: Sorry, we <u>run out of</u> it today. Would you like to try other menu?

A: No, thanks then.

For here or to go? = eat here or to take away?

Run out of: exhaust, use up.

    Cf) I've run out of gas again! / Did we run out of money?

Dialogue 3

A: Hi! How can I help you?

B: Hi! I'd like to order two large pizzas. please.

A: Ok, and what would you like on those pizzas?

B: I'd like one cheese and one… do you have any vegetarian pizzas?

A: Yes, we've got a veggie special pizza. It comes with tomatoes, onions, mushrooms, and green peppers.

B: That sounds wonderful. But can you <u>hold the onions</u>?

A: Sure, no problem. Would you like to add mozzarella cheese on it?

B: Yes. Please.

A: How about something to drink?

B: Large coke please.

Hold the onions: not to add onions.
Hi there, I'd like a double cheeseburger, please. <u>Hold the mustard</u>.

Dialogue 4

A: What can I get for you. sir?

B: I'd like sub. Please.

A: What kind of bread would you like today?

B: I'd like the honey oat.

A: What size sub would you like?

B: I'd like 6 inch.

A: Would you like your bread toasted?

B: Yes, please.

A: What kind of meat?

B: I'd like a Salami please.

A: Would you like cheese? Any extra?

B: a lot of provolone, please.

A: What veggies would you like?

B: I'd love to get everything but hold the cucumbers please.

A: What dressing would you like?

B: I'll go with the honey mustard and a little bit of olive oil, please.

A: Do you want to make it a meal?

B: Yes, I'll have a coke and chips.

A: For here or to go?

B: For here, please.

A: That's good. That comes to 10.50 dollars.

B: Here you go. Thanks.

How to order a subway sandwich?

1. Picking your bread and meat

Select a foot – long or 6-inch sandwich.

Picking your bread – Honey Oat, Italian bread, 9-grain wheat Italian herbs and cheese

Order one of subway's menu items to determine your meat

– Classic Tuna, Rotisserie-style chicken Turkey etc.

2. Adding your toppings

Choose the kind of cheese

– Mozzarella, Cheddar, Pepper jack, Provolone cheese, Swiss cheese,
if you'd like eat your sandwich warm, grill it

Start with large vegetables to add to your sandwich

– Lettuce, tomatoes, cucumbers, peppers, red onions

Cover your larger vegetables with smaller toppings

– pickles, olives, banana peppers, or jalapenos etc.

Choose your sauces based on your preferred flavor.

– Chipotle, Mayonnaise, Ranch, Oil, Vinaigrette, Mustard, etc.

Finish your sandwich with oils or spices if you'd like.

UNIT 5

Asking for directions

  Dialogue 1

A: Excuse me, could you tell me the way to the Fisherman's Wharf?

B: Go straight ahead at the traffic lights, turn left, and keep going straight until you see the sign for the Fisherman's Wharf.

A: How far is it?

B: It's not too far, maybe about 300miters.

A: Oh that's good. thank you very much.

B: You're welcome.

 Dialogue 2

A: Excuse me, how can I get to the post office?

B: Cross the street, you'll find the post office.

A: Thank you.

B: Don't mention it.

Dialogue 3

A: Can you tell me where is the nearest local outdoor market?

B: Go straight ahead and turn right at the <u>intersection</u>. It will be on your right.

A: Thanks a lot.

B: It's nothing.

Dialogue 4

A: Excuse me, sorry to <u>bother</u> you, but would you <u>mind</u> telling me the way to the subway station?

B: Sure, when you get to fifth street, take a left on the traffic lights. It's on the corner. You can't miss it.

A: Thanks.

B: You're welcome. have a good day!

Intersection: crossroads, junction,

    Ex) Turn right at the next intersection with traffic lights.

Bother: annoy, disturb, provoke, inconvenience,

    Ex) Stop bothering me when I'm working.

Do you mind?

    Ex) Do you mind if I open the window?

        Negative answer ‾ Yes

        Positive answer - No

Useful Expression 1

1. Excuse me! Can you tell me the way to the museum?

2. Excuse me! How do I get to the post office?

3. Pardon me! I'm lost. How do I get to the bus station?

4. Excuse me! Is there a convenience store near here?

5. What's the best way to the airport?

6. Excuse me! Could you tell me how to get to subway station?

7. Excuse me! Do you know where the church?

8. Is this the right way to Hilton Hotel?

9. Do you have a city map?

10. Can you show me on the map?

11. Can you give me directions to the nearest bus stop?

12. Where can I find the nearest bakery?

13. Is there a supermarket near here?

14. Can you tell me how to get to the bookstore from here?

15. Excuse me! Where is the restroom?

16. In which direction is the nearest Gas station?

17. Could you please guide me?

18. What direction should I take?

19. What's the quickest way of getting to the supermarket?

20. How do you get to the bus stop?

21. I am looking for this address, am I in the right place?

22. Does this bus go to the city?

23. Sorry to bother you, but would you mind showing me the way to the train station?

24. Can I ask where the Marriott Hotel is?

25. Excuse me! I'm lost. Could you please help me find the 5th Avenue?

26. Excuse me! Can you help me Korea embassy? This is my first time in the city.

27. Sorry to disturb you, but I'm lost. I'm looking for the Big Ben tower.

28. I was wondering if you could help me? I'm looking for the nearest bus stop.

29. Excuse me! Could you tell me where the exchange bank is?

30. Excuse me! Please could you tell me the way to Market street?

31. Do you know where the closest post office is?

32. Am I on the right road to the Mc. Donald?

33. Excuse me! I'm afraid I can't find a gas station.
    Do you know where one is?

34. Will you please tell me where the public restroom is?

35. Would you show me the way to the entrance?

36. How can I find the Italian restaurant?

Useful Expression 2

1. You're going the wrong way.

2. Take the first left.

3. Turn right at the crossroads (intersections).

4. Continue straight ahead for about a kilometer.

5. Continue past the department store.

6. It'll be on your left.

7. It'll be on your right.

8. Take this road.

9. Go down this street.

10. Go straight ahead.

11. Go along the street.

12. It's on the corner, across from the bakery.

13. It's opposite the book store.

14. It's near.

15. Go straight ahead at the traffic lights.

16. Keep going straight ahead, you will find it on the right.

17. Turn right at the junction.

18. Make a left turn when you see the bookstore.

19. Take the first left when you enter fifth Street.

20. Take the fourth exit at the junction and then turn right at the traffic lights.

21. After you pass a restaurant on your left, take a right at the crossroad.

22. Turn left at the end of the corridor.

23. Take a right when you come to the eleventh street.

24. It is behind the supermarket.

25. It is between the post office and the supermarket.

26. It is in front of the bus terminal.

27. It is in the center of the town.

28. Turn right at the intersection and the building is on the right.

29. keep going until you find the sign for the museum.

30. Exit second at the roundabout.

31. Go across the bridge.

32. Go straight and turn right after the gas station.

33. The museum is opposite the railway station.

34. The shop is between the pharmacy and KFC.

35. Drive to Pitt Street and turn left.

36. Go past the cinema and you'll find the library.

37. If you cross the street, you'll see a bookstore there!

38. Is it far from here?

39. It's a long way to walk.

40. It's quite a long way.

41. How far is it to the airport?

42. It's pretty far from here.

43. It's about a mile from here.

44. How long does it take to get there?

45. It takes a while.

46. It takes about a half an hour.

47. It's about a ten-minute walk.

48. If there's no traffic, it's about 25 minutes. In heavy traffic, it takes about 45 minutes.

49. It's about a ten-minute bus ride.

50. How close is it? I'm sorry, I don't know.

51. I'm Sorry, I'm not from around here.

52. I'm afraid I can't help you. You could ask the bus driver.

53. I am stranger here myself.

54. I'm sorry! I have no idea!

55. I'm Sorry. You'll have to ask someone else.

56. You'd better take a taxi.

UNIT
6

Shopping

Dialogue 1

A: Excuse me, can I have a <u>ground beef</u>, please?

B: Here you are. Anything else?

A: Where can I find olive oil?

B: They are in the <u>grocery</u> section over there.

A: Ok, Thank you

Dialogue 2

A: Hello, I'm looking for a shirt.

B: What color would you like?

A: I don't have any idea. what colors have you got?

B: We have got all colors. what about green? I think it matches your blonde hair.

A: Ok, small size please.

B: Yes, here you go.

A: Can I try it on?

B: Sure, the <u>fitting room</u> is over there.

Ground beef: minced beef.

Grocery: grocery store, grocery bag, grocery shopping.

Fitting room: changing room, dressing room.

Dialogue 3

A: Good morning, what can I do for you?

B: Good morning, I'm trying to <u>make up my mind</u> about which kind of dessert to have. Everything looks delicious.

A: Thank you. we have a lot of different types of cakes, cookies, and croissants over there.

B: This blueberry cake looks great. How many people does it served?

A: It has four layers, and it serves between five and six people. <u>Depending on</u> how you slice it.

B: Ok, I'll take it and I'd like five chocolate cookies too.

A: Sure, Would you like the cookies in the same box as the cake?

B: No, please put them in separate box if you don't mind.

A: No problem.

I can't make up mind = I can't decide.

Depend on:

    it depends.

    depend on the weather.

    you can depend on me (you can count on me)

Dialogue 4

A: Good afternoon! can I help you find something?

B: No, thanks, <u>I'm just browsing</u>.

Dialogue 5

A: I'd like to buy this shoes, please.

B: That's $120.

A: Can I pay by credit card?

B: Of course. Please enter your <u>PIN number</u>.

A: Ok. and can I have a <u>receipt</u>, please?

B: Sure, here you are.

A: Thank you.

B: You're welcome. bye

I'm just browsing = I'm just looking around.

PIN: Personal Identification Number.

Receipt:

    Ex) Keep the receipt as proof of your purchase.

Useful Expression

1. What time are you open?

2. We're open from 10am to 8pm, seven days a week

3. What time do you close?

4. How can I help you?

5. I'm just browsing, thank you.

6. I'm Just looking around, thanks.

7. How much is it?

8. That's cheap.

9. That's expensive.

10. I'm looking for a gift.

11. Do you deliver?

12. I'll take it

13. Are you in the queue?

14. I'll pay in cash.

15. I'll pay by credit card.

16. Can I have a receipt, please?

17. Would you be able to wrap it for me?

18. I'd like to change this for a different size.

19. It' doesn't work

20. It doesn't fit.

21. Can I get a refund?

22. Buy onc gct one free.

23. We spent the afternoon window shopping. ex) eye shopping (x)

24. Shopping spree – to spend as much money as possible.

25. Do you think this goes well with my hair?

26. That's a rip off.

27. Is this on sale?

28. Can you do me a deal?

29. Do you offer a student discount?

30. Do you have anything on sale at the moment?

31. Can I return this if I don't like it?

32. Would you like paper or plastic bag?

33. I forgot my reusable bags.

UNIT 7

At the clinic

 Dialogue 1

A: Good morning, Doctor Gunn's office. How may I help you?

B: Good morning, I'd like to make an <u>appointment</u> to see Doctor Gunn,
please.

A: Have you been in to see Doctor Gunn before?

B: No, this is my first time.

A: Ok, what's your name and phone number please?

B: Tom Baker, 010-234-5678 A: Thank you Mr. Baker. What's the reason
for your making an appointment?

B: I have been feeling very bad lately.

A: Do you need <u>urgent</u> care?

B: No, I'm not too much serious, but I'd like to see the doctor soon.

A: Ok, how about next Monday at 11am?

B: That's good. ·

A: Ok, we'll see you next Monday. Goodbye.

B: Thanks, bye.

Appointment: engagement, promise,

    Ex) Previous appointment, break an appointment

Urgent: emergent

    Ex) Is it urgent, it's urgent news,

Dialogue 2

A: Hello, I'd like to make a doctor's appointment.

B: Can you <u>describe</u> your health concern?

A: I have been having <u>cough</u> that aren't going away.

B: Ok, Would Monday or Friday be best for you?

A: I'd like to come in on Friday.

B: I'll put you in for that day at 10am.

　　You can see either Dr. Jason or Dr. Wilson.

A: I'd like to see Dr. Wilson.

B: Ok, see you on Friday.

A: Thank you. bye.

Describe: express, explain,

　　Ex) describe it. try to describe. describe the taste.

Cough:

　　Dry cough / persistent cough / hacking cough

Dialogue 3

A: Come in and sit down please. <u>What's wrong with you</u>?

B: I had a cough and a <u>sore throat</u>.

A: Do you have a <u>fever</u>?

B: I'm not sure. But I feel bad.

A: How long does it last for?

B: Almost a week or so.

A: Let me check your <u>temperature</u> first.

B: Ok.

A: Don't worry. You are just having a cold. Go home to bed and take
a <u>pills</u> three times a day after the meal. You will be fine.

B: Got it. Thank you.

A: Drink more <u>lukewarm</u> water and get a rest.

B: I will. Thank you very much.

What's wrong with you? = What are your symptoms?
Sore throat: pain that worsens with swallowing or talking
Fever: a temporary rise in body temperature.
Pill: tablet, medicine.
　　　Vitamin pill. Sleeping pill.
　　　Take a pill.
　　　'Take a chill pill' = Calm down
Lukewarm: slightly warm,
　　　Cf) Luke warm response

UNIT 8

Pharmacy

Dialogue 1

A: May I help you?

B: I need some medicines.

A: Which medicines do you need?

B: I've got a doctor's prescription.

A: There are four medicines written in this prescription.

B: Please give me the medicines.

A: Anything else?

B: I want some pills for a headache. Have you got a <u>painkiller</u>?

A: Yes, how many tablets do you want?

B: Two packet of ten tablets. Please.

A: Sure, should I make the bill?

B: Yes, please.

A: Here you are.

B: Thank you.

A: Not at all.

Painkiller: a drug that reduces pain, Pain reliever

Dialogue 2

A: Here is your medicine.

B: Thank you very much.

A: Please take 1 tablet three times a day after meals.

These medicines may cause some <u>dizziness and drowsy</u>, when you <u>mix with</u> alcohol so don't drink any alcohol after you take the medicine.

B: I got it.

A: Make sure you take it after eating something.

B: Ok I will. Thanks

A: Sure.

Dizziness: feeling that everything is turning around you. and not able to balance.

Ex) He complained of headaches and dizziness

Drowsy: tired and wanting to sleep. Sleepy

Ex) This tablets may make you fell drowsy.

Mix with something

Ex) I don't like to mix business with pleasure.

Useful Expression

1. I'd like to see a doctor.

2. I'd like to make an appointment to see Dr. Gunn.

3. Do you have medical insurance?

4. What are your symptoms?

5. I've got (a sore throat / headache / stomachache / fever /diarrhea / swollen my ankle / pain in my back ···) I have (a blocked nose / a runny nose) I'm having difficulty breathing.

6. Do you have any allergies?

7. I'm allergic to peanut.

8. Are you on any sort of medication?

9. Blood pressure is very high.

10. Your body temperature is a little high.

11. You need a few stiches.

12. I'll give you an injection / a shot.

13. We need to take your urine sample and blood sample.

14. Can I get a prescription?

15. Does the medication have any side effects?

16. How long will it take to get better?

17. Pharmacy / Pharmacist

18. Over the counter medicine.

19. Pain killer.

20. Antibiotics.

21. Prescription.

UNIT 9

Post Office

 Dialogue 1

A: Good morning, May I help you?

B: Yes, I need to send this package to Seoul.

Which window should I go to?

A: You go to the window marked 'Parcel Post'.

B: Ok, Thank you.

Dialogue 2

A: Excuse me, I need to send this package to Seoul.

B: What does it contain?

A: There are two shirts.

B: Ok, let's see how much it weights. It's about 6 pounds. If you send it express, it will get there tomorrow. Or, you can send it regular and it will get there by Monday.

A: Regular mail is fine. How much will that be?

B: That will be $5.50. Here are your stamps.

A: Thanks.

Parcel: package.

    Ex) there's parcel and some letters for you.

Stamp: ex) He stuck a stamp on the envelope.

UNIT 10

City Tour

Dialogue 1

A: Hello, I'd like to book some tours in this city.

B: Is this your first time in our city?

A: I have been here a couple of years ago but didn't have time to look around.

B: Ok, what type of things you would like to see?

A: I'd like to see all <u>tourist attractions</u> of the city in a day.

B: alright, we do have city tour program and I think you'd like it.

A: I'll take this city tour program please.

B: May I have your name and contact number?

A: John, 010-234-5678.

B: The tour bus picks you up at your hotel front gate at 8am.

A: Ok, thank you.

B: You're welcome.

Tourist attraction: tourist spot.

    Cf) Attraction: interesting or lively place to go or things to do.

    Ex) Buckingham Palace is major tourist attraction.

UNIT 11

Cruise Ship

 Dialogue 1

A: Have you ever travelled on cruise ship?

B: Yes, I have travelled by cruise ship a couple of times.

A: Did you enjoy the cruise trip?

B: Yes, I enjoyed comfortable ship, the blue ocean, the fresh air. And also saw dolphin swimming on the surface of the sea.

A: What is big cruise ship like?

B: The huge cruise ship <u>is equipped with</u> everything from the bed to swimming pool.

A: How many passengers can be on board.

B: Several thousand passengers and together with the crew. There are as many people as in a little town.

A: Where are the <u>cabins</u> and what do they look like?

B: The cabins are above and below deck. The cabin looks like a compartment of a railway sleeping car. Passengers can feel like in a hotel.

A: What can passengers do on a cruise ship?

B: They can enjoy entertaining facilities like movie theater, sports and parties. They can walk on the deck and meet people.

A: That's cool.

UNIT 12

Situational Conversation

 Dialogue 1

A: Are you enjoying your stay in Korea?

B: Very much.

A: Are you with New Zealand Tourism Committee?

B: Yes, we went out to visit several tourist spots in Seoul today.

A: What did you think about it?

B: I think it's very <u>impressive</u>.

Dialogue 2

A: It's so <u>hot and humid</u> outside. I'd like something cool.

B: We have soft drinks and alcoholic beverages.

A: I'll just have a diet coke. Please.

B: Anything else?

A: with some ice please.

B: Sure.

Impressive:

    Ex) That performance was pretty impressive.

    Cf) Impressive speech, first impression

Humid: warm and slightly wet. Muggy, sticky.

    Cf) Humidifier

Dialogue 3

A: This letter goes to Korea.

B: Ok.

A: Do you handle parcels at this window, too?

B: Sorry, please take it to that window over there.

A: Thank you.

B: Next, please.

Dialogue 4

A: Can I get a <u>haircut</u>?

B: How do you want it cut?

A: My hair is too long, <u>trim</u> the sides, but don't touch the top.

B: Ok.

A: Do I pay you?

B: Pay at the counter on your way out, please.

Hair cut: ex) what do you think of my new haircut?

Trim: cut the edge even.

    Trim your hair,

    Cf) Trim any excess fat off the meat.

Dialogue 5

A: I want to try a new hair style.

B: What did you have in mind?

A: Give me a short haircut.

B: How short?

A: I want my hair to be only a few inches long.

B: That's pretty short. Are you sure about this?

A: Yes.

B: Ok, I'll do it.

A: This is what I want.

B: Let's do it.

Useful Expression

1. I don't have an appointment. do you have time today?

2. I'd like a simple haircut.

3. Can I have a shave?

4. Can I request a different shampoo?

5. Could you cut a little bit more?

6. Could you straighten my hair?

7. I'd like to dye my hair.

8. I'd like to change my hair color.

9. What kind of hairstyle do you recommend?

10. Can you show me different hairstyles?

11. Can you make it look like this picture?

12. I'd like a cut and blow dry.

13. Does this price include shampoo?

14. How much do you charge for a cut, wash and blow dry?

15. I'd like a new style / fringe / dry trim / perm.

16. Not too short.

Hairdresser / stylist / Hair salon / barber shop / shampoo / hair dye/ Bleached

Dialogue 6

A: Can I see a memu. Please.

B: Sure. Here it is.

A: What would you recommend?

B: Our specialty is Bulgogi.

A: What's Bulgogi?

B: It's grilled <u>marinated</u> beef in Korea.

 Dialogue 7

A: Look at that long line outside!

B: This is the best Korean restaurant in downtown.

A: <u>It can't be that good</u>!

B: Just wait till you taste their food.

A: What do you usually have for dinner?

B: I usually have shrimp fried rice.

Marinate: Season

　　　Ex) Marinate the meat overnight

　　　Marinate the beef in wine for 30 minutes.

It can't be that good! 저럴 정도로 좋을까?

Dialogue 8

A: Help! Police!

B: What's wrong?

A: MY son is missing. I can't find him anywhere.

B: Ok. What's his name?

A: Tom, He is only 5.

B: Ok. What does he look like?

A: He has brown curly hair. He is tall for his age.

B: What is he wearing today?

A: Jean and white T-shirt. He has a cap on too.

B: How long ago did he go missing?

A: I've been looking for him for almost half an hour now.

B: Where did you last see him?

A: We were just <u>window shopping</u> in the book store.

B: Don't worry. Everything is going to be okay.

A: What should I do?

B: Stay right in the book store in case he comes looking for you.
We'll start looking for him now

Window shopping: browsing, eye shopping(X)

Dialogue 9

A: Hi! What's wrong with you. you look worried.

B: I've lost my passport.

A: Where did you put it?

B: It was my backpack.

A: Have you lost your backpack too?

B: No, It's only the passport.

A: Have you reported it?

B: Not yet.

A: You'd better go to police station.

B: Yes. I will.

A: After the police, you need to tell your embassy too.

B: Ok, thanks.

A: Not at all.

Had better: ex) I'd better get a taxi. The buses are so slow

Embassy: ex) Korean Embassy to US

       Ambassador

       Consul

       Consulate

Dialogue 10

A: Shall we pick several dishes from this menu?

B: Yes, let's see. There are five of us.

A: Let's include seafood.

B: How many dishes shall we order?

A: Let's order <u>enough to go around</u>.

Dialogue 11

A: Excuse me, how much longer will it take?

B: Just a few minutes, sir.

A: We're on a lunch break.

B: Let me check on your order.

A: I'd really <u>appreciate</u> that.

B: Sir, your order will take about ten more minutes.

Enough to go around
    ex) That's more than enough to go around.
Appreciate: be thankful, be grateful.

CHAPTER

5 Food and Beverage

CHAPTER
5 Food and Beverage

The foodservice (US English) or catering (British English) industry includes the businesses, institutions, and companies which prepare meals outside the home.

It includes restaurants, school and hospital cafeterias, catering operations, and many other formats. (Wikipedia)

Food and Beverage Services can be broadly defined as the process of preparing, presenting and serving of food and beverages to the customers.

The food service industry consists of restaurants, travel food service, and vending and contract institutional food service. Local restaurants are made up of establishments that include fast-food units, coffee shop, specialty restaurants, family restaurants, cafeterias, and full-service restaurants with carefully orchestrated "atmosphere."

Travel food service consists of food operations in hotels and motels, roadside service to automobile travelers, and all food service on airplanes, trains, and ships. Institutional food service in companies, hospitals, nursing homes, and so on, is not considered part of the tourism industry.

UNIT 1

Kitchen Tools

1. Chef's Knife: a knife used for preparing food.

   It is used for chopping, slicing, and dicing a variety of food.

2. Spatula: it is for flipping, tossing, and serving all kinds of foods.

3. Whisk: to mix liquid, eggs etc. very quickly so that air is mixed in.

4. Kitchen Shears: Shears are used for heavier cutting than scissors, such as heavy fabric, cardboard, or, in the kitchen, cutting apart meat and bones or tough vegetables, and they do a great job on pizza. Shears can often be taken apart by unscrewing the nut in the center of the pivot for cleaning and sterilizing.

5. Tongs: a type of tool used to grip and lift object instead of holding them directly with hands.

6. Instant read thermometer: used for taking a quick temperature reading of an item, but you don't leave it in the food while it cooks. A meat thermometer is inserted into a piece of meat before roasting and is left in the roast during cooking.

7. Cast-Iron Skillet: Made with thick, heavy bottoms and sides, cast iron pans can evenly heat to high temperatures and retain heat for a long time. Kind of frying pan.

8. Immersion Blender: An immersion blender is a kitchen tool used for blending soups, sauces, and other liquids. An immersion blender is basically a stick with blender blades at the end of it.

9. Colander: A bowl that has many small holes and that is used for washing or drain food such as pasta, vegetables.

10. Cutting Board (or chopping board): a durable board on which to place material for cutting.

11. Apron: is a cloth used by chefs and other cooks to protect their clothing and prevent food and debris from contamination their clothes.

12. Corkscrew: a tool that makes pulling corks from bottles easy.

13. Cutlery: cutlery comprises knives, forks, and spoons. We use them to cut our food into tiny pieces to make it easier to eat them.

14. Dish rack: A dish rack is a kitchen utensil used to hold dishware upright to allow air to circulate to dry or for water to drain.

15. Funnel: A funnel is used to pour liquids into the small openings through its narrow, cylindrical opening.

16. Garlic crusher: crushes garlic with no effort at all.

17. Grater: used for grating and shredding vegetables and other food into fine chucks.

18. Ladle: A large and deep spoon with a long handle that is served for soup or liquid.

19. Lemon squeezer: used to extract the juice from a lemon or other small citrus fruit.

20. Measuring cup: used to measure the amount of liquid or solid ingredients, usually for cooking or baking.

21. Microwave: A type of oven that cooks or heats food very quickly using electromagnetic waves rather than heat.

22. Mortar: a small hard bowl in which you can crush substances such as seeds and grains to make them into powder with a special object, often used in pharmacy.

23. Peeler: a special type of knife for taking the skin off fruit and vegetables "a potato peeler"

24. Peppermill: A hand mill for grinding peppercorns

25. Plate: A plane dish, commonly circular, used in dining service.

26. Potato masher: tool used to mash potatoes.

27. Pressure cooker: A sealed pot in which food can be cooked instantly under steam pressure.

28. Rolling Pin: used for flattening dough or rolls

29. Sieve: Made of a wire or plastic net attached to a ring. The liquid or small pieces pass through the net but the larger pieces do not.

30. Thermos: Keep hot items hot and cold things cold. Thermos can stay hot or cold tea or coffee.

UNIT 2

Cooking Methods

1. **Grilling**: Grilling is one of the popular cooking methods. You can grill anything, from meat, cheese, fruits to vegetables. To grill food, you need to put it directly on an open flame.

2. **Roasting**: The food is exposed to indirect heat from all sides of the oven. People roast meat, such as beef tenderloin, prime rib, pork loin, fruit, and vegetables.

3. **Broiling**: This is the cooking technique that uses radiant heat from above to cook your food, so it's like upside-down grilling.
   Broiling is a good method to use for thinner, leaner cuts of meat like butterflied chicken breasts, pork tenderloin, strip steaks, kabobs and vegetables.

4. Baking: Similar to roasting, baking involves heating the food with indirect heat coming out from all side of oven.

5. Sauteing: To fry food such as small pieces of meat or vegetables in a small amount of fat or oil.

6. Frying: People use this method to make fast food. By emerging the food in boiling oil, it comes out crispy and incredibly delicious.
"Pan-frying and Deep-frying"

7. Searing: Searing is a cooking technique that exposes ingredients (typically meat) to a high temperature to create a crisp browning on the outside. and moist, tender on the inside.

8. Stir-Frying: Stir-frying is a fast and fresh way to cook. Simply toss and turn bite-sized pieces of food in a little hot oil in a wok over high heat, and in five minutes or less, the work is done.
Vegetables emerge crisp and bright. Meats are flavorful, tender, and well seared.

9. Boiling: Boiling is the moist heat method that cooks food in boiling water or other water-based liquids.
Boiled eggs are one of the most common food toppings. You can make hard boiled or soft boiled eggs. Soft boiled eggs have creamy egg yolks, while hard boiled eggs have firm egg yolks.

10. **Steaming**: Steaming is a method of cooking that requires moist heat. The heat is created by boiling water which vaporizes into steam. The steam brings heat to the food and cooks it.

11. **Blanching**: Blanching is the moist heat method by which food is placed in rapidly boiling water for a very short time and is then placed in an ice bath to stop the cooking process. This cooked method is suitable for vegetables, such as asparagus. The aims are to keep the original flavor and texture.

12. **Poaching**: Poaching is a moist heat method of cooking by submerging food in some kind of liquid and heating at a low temperature. It involves submerging the food in hot water rather than boiling water. This is a technique that is used to cook delicate proteins such as fish, chicken, and eggs, as well as some fruits and vegetables.

13. **Simmering**: Simmering is the moist heat method which involves bringing a liquid to just below boiling point while being heated to cook food.

14. **Braising**: the cooking of meat or vegetables by heating them slowly with oil and moisture in a tightly sealed vessel. Braising differs from stewing, in which the food is immersed in liquid, and from covered roasting, in which no liquid is added. Braising is a combination of covered roasting and steaming.

15. Stewing: The procedure of stewing is very similar to braising. The main difference between stewing and braising is that people cut the meat into small pieces in stews, while a braised dish includes large chunks of meat. In addition, people immerse the food partly in the liquid when stewing. But they soak it entirely when braising.

Ingredients

Vegetables

1. **Bulbs**: Usually grow just below the surface of the ground and produce a fleshy, leafy shoot above ground.

   Ex) Garlic, Onion, Leek, Shallot, Spring onion and Fennel

2. **Flowes**: The edible flowers of certain vegetables.

   Ex) Cauliflower, Broccoli, Globe artichoke etc.

3. **Fruits**: Vegetable fruits are fleshy and contain seeds which are sometime eaten.

   Ex) Eggplant, Capsicum, Chili peppers, Tomato, Cucumber, Pumpkin, Buttercup squash, Courgette, Okra, Scallopini, Choke, Melon. Etc.

4. **Fungi**: When referring to vegetables, fungi are commonly known as mushrooms.

     Ex) Button, Crimini, Portabello, Maitake, Hedgehog, Shiitake, Porcini, Lobster, Enoki, Chanterelle, Beech, etc.

5. **Leaves**: The edible leaves of plants.

     Ex) Spinach, Lettuce, Silverbeet, Cabbage, Kale, Salad greens, Herbs, etc.

6. **Roots**: The underground, edible root of a plant that is usually a long or round shaped tap root.

     Ex) Carrot, Turnip, Swede, Beetroot, Celeriac, Daikon radish and Ginger.

7. **Seeds**: Seeds usually grow in pods which are sometimes eaten along with the seeds.

     Ex) Peas, Beans, Snow peas, Sprouted beans, Sweet corn, etc.

8. **Stems**: The edible stalks of plants when the stem is the main part of the vegetable.

     Ex) Asparagus, Celery, Turmeric, Rhubarb, etc.

9. **Tubers**: Vegetables which grow underground on the root of a plant. Tubers are usually high in starch.

     Ex) Kumara, Potatoes, Yam, Taro, Artichokes,

Fishes

1. Carp: A large fish that lives in lakes and rivers, tough flesh and lots of bones

2. Salmon: Born in freshwater, salmon migrate to saltwater and return to their home rivers to spawn. Salmon has a tender texture and mild-to-rich flavor

3. Shad: A herring-like fish that spends much of its life in the sea, it has an oily, mild sweetness, similar to salmon in flavor.

4. Trout: Typically, freshwater fish. Although related to salmon, trout don't have the same pink flesh because their diets are different.

5. Red Snapper: A saltwater fish found off the southeastern coast of the US. real red snapper has red skin and flaky white flesh that tastes mildly sweet.

6. Tuna: The healthy, fresh fish is versatile and easy to grill, bake, and sauté in a flash. 3 ways for cooking (grilling, skillet-cooking, and baking fresh tuna)

7. Cod: Cod is a popular fish known for its mild flavor and dense, flaky flesh. It's one of the most common fish used for making fish and chips.

8. Flounder: is a group of flatfish species. Flounder are versatile fish that can be broiled, sautéd, stuffed and baked, or steamed whole.

9. Catfish: A freshwater fish that's often farmed and sold skinned because its scaleless skin can be difficult to remove. Catfish gets its name from the barbels (fleshy filaments) hanging from its mouth, which look like cats' whiskers.

Meats

1. Pork

Pork is a widely eaten meat, as it comes in various forms, Which makes it more consumable than other varieties of meat. It is easy to prepare, and can have great flavor. Types of pork include bacon, ham, salami, sausages, pancetta, prosciutto, and other products, as well as various cuts of pure pork meat.

2. Beef

Chunk: comes from the cow's shoulder.
- Ground chunk for hamburgers, Shoulder steak, Flat-iron steak, And stew meat.

Rib: Cut from the cow's ribs and backbone. 13pairs of ribs on a cow.
- Short ribs, ribeye steak, cowboy steak, ribeye roast, ribeye filet and back ribs

Loin: The loin is located directly behind the ribs.
- Sirloin is typically best for grilling. "Sirloin steak."
- Short loin is closer to the center of the cow and more tender than sirloin.
  "Tenderloin filet, T-bone, Filet mignon, Porterhouse."

Round: Located near the cow's hind legs. "Round steak"

Frank: Located just below the loin. This region has no bones.
  "Frank steak"

Brisket: belongs to a cow's breast. It is known for its fatty, tough texture.
  "Whole brisket, Brisket flat, Brisket point"

Shank: Located in front of the brisket at the cow's forearm.
  This cut used for stew or soup meat.
  It's best cooked for a long time in moist heat.

3. Veal: Meat from very young cow. Calf meat.

4. Lamb: A young sheep, the flesh of a young sheep eaten as a meat.
   Cf) mutton- the meat from an adult sheep eaten as a meat.

5. Chicken: It is one of the most popular meats around, chicken is a healthier white meat to consume than red meats like beef or lamb.

6. Goat: Goat meat has a strong, gamey flavor, sweeter than lamb but less sweet than beef. Cooking it with lots of flavor and spices helps complement its unique flavor.

7. Turkey: Low in fat and richer in protein than chicken, turkey is a lean meat and a good choice for those looking to reduce their fat intake. However, its high protein, low fat content means the meat can cook quickly and become dry.

8. Pheasant: The taste of any pheasant's meat will depend mainly on whether it is wild or farm-raised. Farm-raised pheasant has a very light and clean taste to it, very similar to the white meat from chicken. It may have a slightly gamey tone depending on how it was raised.

9. Duck: Duck is packed with essential nutrients, lean like chicken, can have fewer calories than other poultry.

Others

1. **Grains**: Wheat, Oats, Rice, Corn, Barley, Millet, Rye, Sorghum Buckwheat,

2. **Beans**: Soybeans, Red beans, Mung beans, peas.

3. **Seaweed**: Laver, Brown seaweed, Sea lettuce

4. **Soy sauce**: Traditionally made from a fermented paste of soybeans, roasted grain, and used for seasoning for food.

5. **Soybean paste**: A type of fermented bean paste made entirely of soybean. It is also a byproduct of soy sauce production.

6. **Red pepper paste**: Red chili paste that also contains glutinous rice, fermented soybeans, salt. It's a thick and spicy sauce. It can be used for variety of dishes, from soups, meat stews, fish, steak, chicken.

7. **Garlic**: A plant of the onion family that has a strong taste and smell and is used in cooking to add flavor. Minced garlic is used for seasoning.

8. **Mustard**: It is commonly paired with meats, vegetables and cheeses, especially as a condiment for sandwiches, hamburgers, and hot dogs.

9. Cinnamon: Cinnamon is one of the world's most popular spices, sprinkled on lattes, boiled with ciders and enjoyed in numerous dishes. Without it, Thanksgiving and Christmas meals might well become tasteless and definitely less fragrant.

10. Edible oil: Most common vegetable oils include soybean oil, sunflower, corn, olive, sesame, wild sesame, and coconut oil.

11. Vinegar: It is now mainly used in the culinary arts as a flavorful, acidic cooking ingredient or in pickling. Various types of vinegar are also used as condiments or garnishes, including balsamic vinegar and malt vinegar.

UNIT 4

Restaurant Equipment

Ovens

1. Radiant(standard) oven: Basic oven that heat up from the bottom.

2. Convection oven: This oven is equipped with a fan that circulate air, which help cook food evenly all the way through while still maintaining its flavor.

3. Steam oven: This fast-cooking oven uses water vapor to cook food. It also cooks evenly, but can't make food crispy.

4. Combination oven: A combi oven is a three-in-one oven which allows you to cook with steam, hot air(convection) or a combination of both.

5. Conveyor oven: Similar to a convection oven, but moves food through one side to another where it comes out cooked. Great for pizza.

6. Microwave oven: This is one of the most common types of equipment used in a restaurant kitchen for finishing touches or single servings. With a microwave, you can reheat pre-made dishes in no time.

Ranges and Ventilation

1. Induction

is performed using direct induction heating of cooking vessels, rather than relying on indirect radiation, convection, or thermal conduction. Induction cooking allows high power and very rapid increases in temperature to be achieved, and changes in heat settings are instantaneous.

2. Ventilation

A Type 1 exhaust hood has a built-in fire prevention system to tackle broiling, frying, and grilling, while a Type 2 hood is better suited to baking and steaming.

3. Food processors

Slice, chop, grind, puree, grate, and dice – all with one piece of restaurant equipment.

4. Mixers

A commercial floor mixer is a necessary piece of equipment in any bakery, restaurant, pizzeria, or other establishment that makes dough and batter in-house.

5. Slicers

a tool or machine for slicing partitular types of food. (Bread slicer, Meat slicer)

6. Sharpening Stones

longstanding tool used to sharpen blades by grinding them against an abrasive surface.

7. Ice makers

  ice generator or ice machine for making ice

8. Gas or Electric grill

  gas grills are the outdoor cooking appliances fueled by propane or natural gas.

9. Griddle

  is a cooking device consisting mainly of a broad, usually flat cooking surface. Nowadays it can be either a movable metal pan - or plate - like utensil.

10. Deep Fryer

  for deep fried staples like French fries, onion rings, or jalapeño poppers.

11. Pre counters and cutting boards

  It's important to invest in the proper materials needed for restaurant business to make your food prep as sanitary as possible.

  Wood is very unsanitary – especially when working with meat and poultry – so you'll want to choose a stainless steel prep table and high-density polyethylene cutting board instead.

12. Fridges and Freezers

  fridges - keep your food cold and fresher for longer (refrigerator) / freezers - food frozen at extremely low temperatures.

13. Sinks

a sink is plumbing fixture for washing hands, dishwashing, and other purposes.

14. Storage Racks and Shelving

Air drying racks, utility carts, and shelves are all key items to keep your restaurant from looking like a tornado blew through. When storing items on shelves, make sure to keep the things you use most close to ground level, rather than high up, so they're easily accessible.

15. Safety Equipment

A first-aid kit is one of the must-have materials needed in a restaurant. It has to be accessible in the workplace at all times, along with a fire extinguisher.

16. Kitchen Display System(KDS)

Link this tool to your front of house point of sale system to make it easier for kitchen staff to manage incoming orders.

17. Point of Sale(POS)

A POS system allows your business to accept payments from customers and keep track of sales.

A point-of-sale system used to refer to the cash register at a store.

Today, modern POS systems are entirely digital, which means you can check out a customer wherever you are. All you need is a POS app and an internet-enabled device, such as a tablet or phone.

Dialogue

Dialogue at Steak House

    A: Good evening, welcome to K- Steakhouse, I will be your server tonight.

    B: Hello, how are you?

    A: I am great, thank you for asking, can I get you started with something to drink?

    B: Yes, can we get two red wines and water please?

    A: Sure, I will be right back with your drinks.

    B: Thank you, and can we get an extra menu as well?

    A: Certainly! (she leaves...)

    A: Here is your wine. Are you ready to order?

    B: Yes, we are. What does the T-bone steak come with?

    A: It comes with veggies and mashed potatoes.

    B: Okay, I will have the T-bone steak.

    A: Of course, and how would you like your steak cooked?

    B: Well done, please.

    A: Sure, how about you ma'am?

    B: Can I have Caesar salad with chicken, please?

    A: Absolutely. And for the little guy?

    B: We will have macaroni and cheese for him?

    A: Sure! And would you like anything to drink mister?

B: Just water Please.

A: Great! I will be back with your orders.

B: Perfect...

A: Here are you orders! Enjoy your meal...

A: How is everything so far?

B: Great thanks, can we get the check, please?

A: Certainly...

A: Here is your bill, you can pay at the cashier whenever you are ready.

B: Thank you.

A: Thank you, enjoy the rest of your evening.

Korean Cuisine

CHAPTER

6

Korean Cuisine

Korean cuisine has evolved through centuries of social and political change. Originating from ancient agricultural and nomadic traditions in Korea and southern Manchuria, Korean cuisine reflects a complex interaction of the natural environment and different cultural trends. Korean cuisine is largely based on rice, vegetables, seafood and (at least in South Korea) meats. Dairy is largely absent from the traditional Korean diet. Traditional Korean meals are named for the number of side dishes (banchan) that accompany steamcooked short-grain rice. Kimchi is served at nearly every meal.

Commonly used ingredients include sesame oil, deonjang (fermented beanpaste), soysauce, salt,garlic, ginger, gochugaru (pepper flakes), gochujang (fermented red chili paste) and Napa cabbage. (Wikipedia)

Korean table manners

The Koreans eat with spoons and chopsticks. How to use chopsticks can be briefly explained as follows: you hold the upper stick between your thumb and first two fingers, while you keep the lower stick stationary with your third finger or both your second and third finger. Korean restaurant will usually bring you a pair of wooden half-split chopsticks in paper envelopes. You can easily split them into two. In Korean homes, however, permanently reusable steel sticks are used.

The spoon is for your rice and soup, and your chopsticks are for everything else.

In Korea, dining etiquette differs from that practiced in the West.

For example, it is entirely acceptable to make slurping noises from time to time, while eating noodles with chopsticks. This is not taken to be bad table manners as in the West.

UNIT 1

Korean meals

1. Soup

In the Korean meal, soup is eaten simultaneously with (not prior to) the main course (rice and other side dishes). In western style restaurants, however, you can have western style soups.

2. Salad

Salad isn't part of Korean cuisine. Pickled vegetables are a more typical equivalent. However, you can order salads in western style restaurants.

3. Bulgogi

Barbecued beef or pork that marinated with soy sauce, sesame oil, minced garlic, black pepper, green onions, and toasted sesame seeds. It is charcoal

- broiled over a grill.

4. Kimchi

Kimchi was created as a way to preserve vegetables for the winter months. There are more than 100 different types of kimchi. The most common types of kimchi served are Baechu kimchi, Kkakdugi, and Nabak kimchi.

What started as cabbage simply pickled in salty brine slowly transformed into the kimchi we know today, through the addition of various spices and seasonings such as hot pepper powder.

There are many variations in recipes and forms, using different vegetables such as cabbage, radish, and cucumber. The health benefits of kimchi have been scientifically proven, increasing the global interest in this Korean food. household kimchi refrigerators are more commonly used.

5. Samgyeopsal

pork strips sizzling on a grill. Served with lettuce, perilla leaves, sliced onions and raw garlic kimchi, it's smudged in ssamjang (a mix of soybean paste called 'doenjang' and chili paste called 'gochujang') or salt and pepper in sesame oil. (CNN travel)

6. Chimaek

Chimaek, short for "chicken, maekju (beer)" is actually not a dish, but an institution. This glorious pairing features two surprisingly mundane foods: fried chicken and beer. (CNN travel)

7. Kimchi Stew

In kimchi-jjigae, red cabbage kimchi is chopped, sauteed in oil, and cooked with tofu, pork (sometimes tuna), and other vegetables. (CNN travel)

8. Tteokbokki

Tteokbokki is a simple Korean street food snack made of rice cakes and fish cakes. This iconic street food is so popular there's an entire part of Korea just devoted to the steamed and sliced rice cakes (tteok), cooked with fish cakes and scallions in a sweet and spicy sauce made of chili paste. (CNN travel)

9. BiBimbab

This Korean lunch-in-a-bowl mixes together a simple salad of rice, mixed vegetables, rice, beef, and egg, with sesame oil and a dollop of chili paste for seasoning. (CNN travel)

10. Kimbap

Sauteed vegetables, ground beef, sweet pickled radish, and rice, rolled and tightly wrapped in a sheet of laver seaweed (Gim), and then sliced into bite-sized circles. (CNN travel)

11. Sundubu Jjigae (Soft Tofu Stew)

Soft tofu, clams and an egg in spicy broth? The soft tofu - which breaks into fluffy chunks in the stew- holds the flavor of the clam and serves as a relief from the overall spiciness. Proper sundubu-jjigae comes in a traditional earthenware pot designed to retain heat. The egg is cracked into the stew after serving, and cooks inside the bowl. (CNN travel)

12. Maeuntang

Usually, in a Korean restaurant, the spicy fish stew will be labeled 'Maeuntang'. Maeuntang is made with cod, but the soup can be made with any fish.

13. Samgyetang

Chicken ginseng soup. Chicken stuffed with glutinous rice, ginseng, and dried jujube, steamed and served hot.

14. Mandu

Dumplings. Meat, vegetables and sometimes soybean curd, stuffed into a dumpling and steamed, fried, or boiled in a broth.

15. Momilguksu

Buckwheat noodles served with a sweet soy radish sauce.

16. Naengmyeon

Cold buckwheat flour or potato flour noodles topped with sliced meat, vegetables, boiled egg, pepper relish sauce and ice.

UNIT 2

Street food in Korea

In South Korea, inexpensive food may be purchased from 'Pojangmacha', street carts during the day, where customers may eat standing beside the carts or have their food wrapped up to take home. At night, 'Pojangmacha' become small tents that sell food, drinks, and alcoholic beverages. (Wikipedia)

1. Hotteok

Korean sweet pancakes (Hotteok) are one of the most popular Korean street snacks. They are particularly popular in winter. It's crispy outside and inside is filled with sweet gooey indulgence.

2. Bungeoppang

It is a fish shaped pastry that is particularly popular in winter streets of Korea.

The fish shaped pastry are often filled with something inside.

Back in the days, the only available fillings were sweetened red bean paste.

But, nowadays, you have more choices.

3. Eomuk

Fishcakes are called Eomuk, fish cakes are mainly made of corvine or cuttlefish which contains less fat.

4. Sundae

The Sundae is one of the most popular street food specialties of Korea, ready to be eaten at the street stalls or in the various restaurants. It is s stuffed blood sausage appreciated by the local population. The typical Korean food is usually made by filling the intestines of a cow or a pig with Dangmyeon(potato noodles), offal and pig's blood. Everything then steamed or boiled in a pot giving the Sundae a solid consistency similar to the sausage.

5. Dak-Kkochi

Korean chicken skewers consisting of grilled small pieces of chicken It's often coated with thick, sticky, and addictive sauce. Some sauces are sweet and salty and some are sweet and spicy.

6. Gyeran-Ppang

"egg bread" today. This is a sweet, steamy, hot and fluffy little loaf of bread with a whole egg inside. It's sold by street vendors all over Korea.

UNIT 3

Korean Restaurants

Most restaurants are open for lunch and dinner, often with a 3pm to 5pm hiatus in the afternoon, Restaurants with night-time entertainment usually start their live music at 8pm, and they often close after midnight.

1. Barbecue meat restaurants (Bulgogijip)

   Beef(Sogogi), Pork(Deojigogi) and short rib(Galbi) are marinated in soy sauce, sesame oil, garlic, green onions, and toasted sesame seeds, then char-broiled.

2. Raw fish restaurants (Saengson Hoejip)

   Sliced fresh raw fish is served with a soy sauce or red pepper sour sauce.

Other fish dishes include Maeun-tang(Hot pepper soup of fish, soybean curd, egg, and vegetables)

3. Ginseng Chicken Soup restaurants(Samgyetangjip)

Chicken stuffed with rice, white ginseng, and dates are steamed and served hot. Deep-fried chicken is also served.

4. Dumpling restaurants(Mandujip)

Meat, vegetables, and sometimes tofu are stuffed into dumplings and steamed, fried, or boiled in a broth. Chinese-style pastries baked in the restaurant are also sold.

5. Noodle restaurants(Bunsikjip)

Noodle dishes are the specialty but so are simple rice dishes.

Some of the popular dishes are Momil guksu-buckwheat noodles with a sweet radish sauce.

Naengmyen − cold potato flour or buckwheat flour noodles topped with sliced meat, vegetables, a half boiled egg, and a pepper relish sauce.

Kongguksu − wheat noodles in fresh soya milk.

Eomuk guksu − wheat noodles topped with oriental fishcake in a broth.

Ramyeon − instant noodles in instant broth.

Udong − wide wheat noodles with onions, fried tofu, red pepper powder, and egg.

Bibimbap − rice topped with various vegies like parboiled fern bracken, bluebell root, beansprouts, spinach, fried egg, and seasoned red pepper paste, accompanied by a warming bowl of broth

6. Basic Korean meal restaurants(Baekbanjip)

Rice is served with a variety of side dishes Kimchi, Namul(parboiled vegetables), fish and soup.

7. Japanese restaurants

Complete with susi, sashimi, and tempura(deep-fried battered fish and vegetables) are all over Korea, and are even more common in the southern port of Busan, Japanese restaurants tend to be on the pricey side, but affordable sushi places are now appearing in office workers' areas of cities to serve the lunch-time crowd.

Bar in Korea

A Korean style bar is a place that serves drinks with food. The main focus of these places is drinking and hanging out with friends.

So what can you expect from Korean style bars? They are usually called 'Suljip' which literally means 'alcohol house. These places have an open plan bar with simple tables and seats. For people having parties or in a large group, Hof bars and 'Suljips' are great places to visit. The food served here varies from place to place, but the most common food is fried chicken or some kind of meat dish.

1. Soju

Is a clear and colorless Korean distilled alcoholic beverage. Soju is the best selling liquor in Korea.

Its alcohol content varies from about 12.9% to 53% alcohol by volume(ABV), although since 2007 low alcohol soju below 20% has become more popular. While soju is traditionally made from the grain of rice, wheat, or barley, modern producers often replace rice with other starches, such as potato and sweet potato. (Wikipedia)

2. Makgeolli

Korean rice wine The milky, off-white, and lightly sparkling rice wine has a slight viscosity that tastes slightly sweet, tangy, and bitter.

As a low proof drink of six to nine percent alcohol by volume, it is often considered a "communal beverage" rather than hard liquor.

Recently, various fruits such as strawberries and bananas are added to Makgeolli to drink in new forms. (Wikipedia)

UNIT 5

Korean Cafe Culture

If you really like coffee, tea, or various tasty beverages, then you should visit Korea for understanding its coffee culture and experiencing different coffee shops. At first, let's look into how Korea's love affair with coffee has been started. Coffee has been one of the most attractive beverages in Korean culture for the last several decades. If you want coffee or other beverages, you can simply go into any coffee shop on your way. It is amazing because every coffee shop has its own unique atmosphere and design. You can spend time there enjoying coffee, reading a book, doing your homework, chatting with friends, working on the laptop or just sitting and enjoying the day with every sip of coffee. (Artur Tron)

Korean coffee culture is defined by its variety. This variety spans over the type of cafes and also the coffee menu.

Cafes, with their great ambience, became the great place for friends to come together and catch up over a cup of coffee.

UNIT 6

Holiday food in Korea

1. Tteokguk (rice cake soup)

Tteokguk, a Korean rice cake soup, is a must-have for the first day of the Lunar New Year, called Seollal.

It is tradition to eat tteokguk on New Year's Day because it is believed to grant the people good luck for the year and gain a year of age.

Chewy oval rice cakes are simmered in a light beef broth and topped with shredded brisket, thin ribbons of egg omelet, fragrant scallions, and roasted seaweed. It's a comforting dish to welcome in the new year.

2. Songpyeon (Half-moon shaped rice cake)

Songpyeon is traditionally eaten during the Korean autumn harvest festival, Chuseok.

Chuseok is often referred as the Korean Thanksgiving, although it comes a little earlier in the year and has just as much in common with the harvest festival seen in other countries all over the world.

Songpyeon is a must-have Chuseok delicacy. These small halfmoon shaped rice cakes are stuffed with sweet fillings such as sweetened sesame seeds and traditionally steamed on a bed of pine needles. The name Songpyeon stems from the use of pine needles, because "song" in "Songpyeon" means pine tree.

3. Jeon

Sanjeok, or skewers made with beef marinated in soy sauce, and other colorful vegetables, are some of the basics.

Jeon, often referred to as small pancakes, are also popular. Each household usually cooks more than one kind of 'Jeon' : they make 'Dongreurrnagttaeng', a type of meat ball, 'Hobak Jeon', made with zucchini, or 'Pajeon with green scallions etc.

4. Namul

Marinated vegetables called 'Namul' are also a must. 'Gosari(fern), 'Sigeumchi (spinach), radish, and 'Doragi (balloon flower roots) are a few of the commonly made 'Namul' at home

5. Dongji Patjuk (red bean porridge with rice ball)

'Patjuk' is a type of Korean 'Juk' (porridge) consisting of red beans and rice ball. It is commonly eaten during the winter season in Korea, and is associated to 'dongji' (winter solstice) as people used to believe that the red color of Patjuk drives off baneful spirits.

As the day with the shortest daylight hours and the longest night, 'Dongji' has traditionally been considered to be a day full of negative energy. Our ancestors ate red bean porridge on the day of the Winter Solstice (Dongji) because they believed the red beans had the power to chase away evil spirits. The color of the red bean was believed to symbolize positive energy.

CHAPTER

7

E-Mails and Letters

CHAPTER
7   E-Mails and Letters

1

Greetings Jinoh,

Thanks for your email.

Here's my number : 222-3333

Please call between 22.00 and 23.00 on Monday, Wednesday or Friday. Alternatively, you can call in the afternoon about 12.30

Take care,

(2)

Greetings Jin-oh,

How're you? Did you manage to get home before the next day?

How about Tom? When I left both of you at Wanju-gun I realized it was 11.00pm and had sympathy.

Anyway, tell me when you're ready for Taedunsan. I can't recall your next free Saturday.

Take care and God bless.

Ritchie

③

Hi Jinoh,

How have you been? Did you manage to obtain any info on Cheju?

I hope you'll get this message as the computers may not be working.

Take care,

Ritchie

Anyonghaseyo!

How have you been? I trust alright.

Please remind when you'll be in Kyongju. I recall it's next month but I've forgotten the dates.

In addition, please let me know when you're available for Namwon particularly Chirisan. The weather is getting cooler so I guess the conditions will be much favorable for hiking.

I trust you had an enjoyable chusok!

Anyonghi kaseyo.

⑤

Hey Jinoh,

Thanks for your email. Good to hear from you.

Regarding Chusok, Japan was fine despite some hitches.

I trust your Chusok was memorable.

I guess both dates are suitable for Chirisan Oct 14 and Oct 21.

I was thinking of choosing Oct 21 as Yongho's wedding is on Oct 22.

Do you think it's possible to hike Chirisan and attend a wedding the following day? You know all about Namwon so I'll welcome your advice.

Perhaps, I'll drop-in on tomorrow, Lord willing.

Thanks for the correction. Anyonghi kyeseyo

Hi! Jinoh

how are you doing? how's the weather in Korea?

I just want to say happy holidays and have a great lunar New Year.

I hope the coming new year will bring health and wealth to you and your family.

I will talk to you soon.

Lawrence.

7

Greetings Jinoh!

I trust you're doing fine.

Just a little query. Do you know the schedule for flights from Kunsan to Chejudo starting from the eve of January 22 to January 25? I would appreciate receiving such information at your earliest opportunity.

Well, we're living in the 21st century, aren't we? May I use this opportunity to wish you well.

May you really be blessed throughout this new year!

Hi Jinoh,

Do they have flights around 10pm on Jan 22? If not, what about morning flights on Jan 23?

I'll call you today after work around 7pm.

Bye for now

9

Greetings Jinoh,

I left the U.K. last month to Japan where I stayed for a while. Then I had to travel to Kurye for some meetings.

There's a lot going on but I'm ok. I trust you're much better.

Remember my laptop! I'm trying to connect it to the internet so I don't have to go those PC centres to inhale their cigarette smoke.

Once I get it set up, it'll be much easier to keep in touch.

By the way, any great plans?

Bye for now.

Hi Jinoh,

How have you been?

I trust the atmosphere at work is improving.

Please could you do me a favor. Do you know the names of those big travel agencies? I believe they're Hana and Modu. Do they organize package tours to Thailand/Australia/New Zealand?

Looking forward to hear from you.

Take care,

11

Hi Jinoh!

How are you getting on?

Regarding the visa issue, I was quite astonished by the response of Modu tour.

I know a fellow British citizen who recently went to both Australia and New Zealand. He didn't require a visa.

I therefore called the embassies to verify. The New Zealand embassy stated "NO VISA IS REQUIRED FOR U.K. CITIZENS FOR UP TO THREE MONTHS PARTICULARLY IF THE TRAVELLER HAS A ROUNDTRIP TICKET" They like to know your return date to confirm how long you're staying in their country.

I called the Australian embassy too, but they don't take telephone enquiries in the morning. Nonetheless, I believe it's the same.

Jinoh, Modu tour have got it wrong here. They can call the embassies if they need further confirmation.

I trust all's well in Chonju.

God bless,

⑫

Oh sorry! I forgot to mention this. I don't have a fax machine so I have to send the passport photocopy by registered post.

I trust you receive it in good time.

Cheers,

13

Thanks Jinoh for the invitation.

I was about to email you before receiving your message. I trust you're doing fine.

It would be great to see a taekwondo competition in Chonju. I haven't seen that before. Lord willing, I would endeavor to stop by your office at 1pm tomorrow. By the way, do you know where I can access the email addresses of Korean Embassies or Consulates in Europe? Secondly, have you come across the email addresses or websites of the following travel agencies - Top Travel, Hana and Modu. I heard they are big agencies in Seoul.

Have a lovely day and see you tomorrow!

14

Hello Jinoh,

How're things? I believe all is well.

Just to inform you that I won't be coming to your office on Saturday. If you recall, we were supposed to finalize arrangements to Taejon next Saturday.

I'll suggest that we meet at Express bus terminal instead of your office. As for time, I've not made up my mind. Tell me what you think. You could drop me an email or call me on Monday.

Take care and God bless

Hi Jinoh,

How are things? I trust all is well.

Did you manage to obtain information on the ferry to China from Kunsan and to Japan too? If you did, you could email me. Maybe they have package tours which are better than those I showed you last weekend.

By the way, anything on our next destination or you've not decided yet? Please keep me informed particularly about the city tour buses.

Just like you said, the full day tour bus is the easiest way of getting around a new town.

Take care and see you.

(16)

Hi Jinoh,

Thanks for your email and the info included.

19.25pm is a difficult time for me. I usually finish my last class at 6.45pm which hardly leaves any time to get there. Don't they have flights at a much later time on Jan 22, say between 9-11pm? If not, do they have flights on Jan 23 particularly in the morning?

As for the return, 8.45am is too early to leave Jeju airport. Don't they have flights in the evening?

Finally, do you know how long it takes to get to Kunsan airport and how much it will cost?

Once again, thanks Jinoh! I appreciate your assistance and await your reply.

Take care,

Thanks again for your help Kim Jin Oh.

I am looking forward to the weekend. My friends and I have booked a condo for 2 nights. The complex has a pool, spa and sauna, so we are going to chill out, watch video's, play something and perhaps drink a little!

And so, to do this, I need to catch the bus to Seoul.

What are your plans? Are you going visiting?

I have learnt how to say 'happy new year' in Korean, however I can't write it!

So Happy New Year!

No doubt, I will be harassing you again soon for information.

Take it Easy, Amy

(18)

Good Afternoon,

Do you know the names or how to make arrangements for tours that go to the DMZ? We are hoping to go the weekend of August 10th. Are you able to help? Thanks for all your help on Sunday. It was a really fun day. I have pictures from that day.

My hours at work have changed, so I am not able to come by and visit until summer break is over. I will show the pictures to you then.

You had mentioned that you were interested in going to Muju or Jirisan. When would be a good time for you? I'd like to start planning my weekend trips.

Hope you are well,

Heather

Hello Jinoh,

Thanks a million for your help. I have a couple of questions still.

A: How many people would we be able to put into a room in the MinBak? (there may be six or more people travelling in our group).

B: Are there shuttle buses running from the MinBak to the resort, or how close is the MinBak to the resort?

C: Are there buses running from Seoul to Muju on the morning of January 30th? Where do they leave from?

D: Is it possible to get a reduction on the lift pass or equipment rental if we are a group (of 6-8 people) and if we will be skiing there for 4 or 5 days?

Once again, thank you very much for all of your help.

I hope to hear from you soon,

Kind Regards,

Mitchell

Hi Jin-Oh

A group of us is planning a trip to Gyeongju on the Oct. long weekend. We want to catch an early bus on Friday morning to get there. Can you pls. tell me what the morning bus schedule is to Gyeongju.

Thank you, Ruth

21

Hi all Since next week is Heather's birthday, I'd like to organize a party for her next Wed. night. Can you make it? I'd like to get together at a bar where there's enough room for all of us and where we can be loud (i.e. not Lavazza - it's a great bar but pretty quiet). Perhaps the Underground at Chon Buk Uni.? I'm suggesting 9:00 or 9:15 so we can all be there before Heather arrives. Unless you could arrange to come with her at about 10:00 Brendan?... I'll bring a cake. Hope you can come - let me know.

Cheers, Ruth

(22)

Dear Jin Oh,

Hope this email finds you in good health.

Thank you very much for your brochures which we received yesterday. It was very informative and our agents are all ready to promote it.

KNTO Singapore office is also very excited. They might do a writeup on the annual travel fair (NATAS) newspaper supplement in October thus we need more brochures or information to provide to the journalists. Hence, we would really appreciate if your office can send us about 50 copies each or more of the brochures as we will also be promoting it in Malaysia. big brochure (Jeonju Traditional Culture Center) is most helpful.

Also, we understand that a new drama, Summer Scent, is being filmed right now. Would appreciate any information that you may have or list of filming areas in Jeollabuk-do so that we may plan future itineraries to visit those places, just like how Nami Island got so popular after Winter Sonata.

As for the Jeonju Sori Festival, the timing clashes with our annual school examinations period. Our school term starts in January and ends in mid-November thus September and October is our 'low' season. However, I'll still put up notices to related parties to draw interest and awareness.

Meanwhile, please do not hesitate to contact my colleague, Mr Jason Luan in our Seoul office should you have any queries. you may reach us at this email.

We really appreciate your kind assistance and support. Wishing you well always.

Thank you and best regards,

Jasmine

[Reference]

1. Setupmyhotel.com

2. https://www.thoughtco.com

3. https://www.englishclub.com/english-for-work/airlineannouncements.htm

4. https://airlinecareer.com

저자 소개

Jin-oh Kim

Jeonbuk National University graduate school (Master of English linguistics)

현) President of Global Korea co. Ltd.
  Lecturer of Jeonju University
  Inspector of Hotel grade evaluation
  Consultant of Tourism DURE

전) Adjunct Professor of Jeonju Kijeon College
  Visiting Professor of Woosuk University
  Branch Director of Chongro Overseas Educational Institute
  English Speaking Information Officer for Inbound Tourism

[Specialty]
- Specialist of English Camp in New Zealand, Canada, Australia etc.
- English Tour Guide license for Foreign Tourist
- English Interpreter of Tourism Business
- Tour Conductor
- Facilitator

[Thesis]
- A Sociolinguistic study of apartment brand in Korea

저자와의
합의하에
인지첩부
생략

Global Service English

2023년 1월 10일 초판 1쇄 인쇄
2023년 1월 30일 초판 1쇄 발행

지은이 김진오
펴낸이 진욱상
펴낸곳 백산출판사
교 정 박시내
본문디자인 오행복
표지디자인 오정은

등 록 1974년 1월 9일 제406-1974-000001호
주 소 경기도 파주시 회동길 370(백산빌딩 3층)
전 화 02-914-1621(代)
팩 스 031-955-9911
이메일 edit@ibaeksan.kr
홈페이지 www.ibaeksan.kr

ISBN 979-11-6639-301-3 93740
값 18,000원